CHRISTIANITY
in ROMAN
BRITAIN

CHRISTIANITY in ROMAN BRITAIN

David Petts

TEMPUS

First published 2003

PUBLISHED IN THE UNITED KINGDOM BY:
Tempus Publishing Ltd
The Mill, Brimscombe Port
Stroud, Gloucestershire GL5 2QG

PUBLISHED IN THE UNITED STATES OF AMERICA BY:
Tempus Publishing Inc.
2 Cumberland Street
Charleston, SC 29401

British Library Cataloguing in Publication Data.
A catalogue record for this book is available from the British Library.

ISBN 0 7524 2540 4

Typesetting and origination by Tempus Publishing.
Printed in Great Britain by Midway Colour Print, Wiltshire.

CONTENTS

INTRODUCTION

This book was mostly written in York, the town in which Constantine was raised to the purple on the death of his father in AD 306. A statue of him now stands outside York Minster, a site that has seen Christian worship for well over a millennium. The focus of my academic work, which I began in York, has always involved the study of Christianity in its earliest guises. The thrust of my work has previously centred on the early medieval period; however, the more I studied this period the more important I realised it was to really get to grips with the origins and nature of Romano-British Christianity. Anyone who has studied this phenomenon will always turn to Charles Thomas' *Christianity in Roman Britain to AD 500*, a work for which the 'magisterial' is rightly always used. Thomas carefully analysed the archaeological and historical evidence for the Church in Britain in this early period. The book I have written is certainly not intended to replace it, and, whilst I have not always agreed with some of the arguments presented in it, it is still the first book I turn to when exploring a new aspect of the Church. However, over the twenty years since it was published important new discoveries and approaches in the archaeology of early Christianity have been made. Many of these new finds, as well as reassessments of earlier discoveries have been more recently critically re-examined in Frances Mawer's *Evidence for Roman Christianity in Britain: The Small Finds*, which is essential reading for anybody who wished to pursue this topic further. Rather than presenting extensively every single example of possible or probable evidence for Christianity in Roman Britain I have tried to make this a book of synthesis. Whilst, as Romanists never fail to point out to me, the archaeological evidence for the religion in Britain is not extensive, there is enough data to allow important things to be said about the nature of late Roman religion and society. I am sure some people will not agree with many of the arguments put forward in this book, but it is important to move the study of Romano-British Christianity forwards from an exercise in data collection and to try and integrate it thoroughly with study of Late Antique Britain.

Many of the ideas in this book have been slowly coming together over the last ten years, and have been closely related to arguments I have developed on work I have done on early medieval Christianity. It would be invidious to try and list every single person who has helped form these ideas in conversations in pubs, common rooms and conferences over the last decade. However, several people deserve a special mention for either letting me see unpublished work or providing insightful but friendly criticism of my ideas: Ken Dark, Dominic Perring, Howard Williams and Sam Turner. I would also like to particularly mention Martin Henig, who, perhaps unknowingly, got me interested in Roman religion, and has always been willing to offer friendly help and advice ever since. Two people who sadly are not able to see the publication of this book are my grandmother Kathleen Taggart and my great aunt Grace Gough, by whose help I was able to finish my academic study. Finally I would like to take this opportunity to thank my parents, Jim and Catherine, and my sister Caite, who have always been a great support through my archaeological career. This book would never have been finished without the love and support of my partner Jane, and it is to her I dedicate it.

1

LOOKING AT CHRISTIAN
ROMAN BRITAIN

When the Roman legions first landed in Britain they were invading a country with a rich and profoundly powerful religion. Julius Caesar had already been impressed by the power of the Druids during his campaigns in Gaul. A century later the Roman general Agricola confronted the political power of native British religion when he attacked the Isle of Anglesey, the stronghold of the druids in Britain. Like all invading powers the Roman occupation involved not just the creation of an apparatus of political and economic power, but the imposition of new structures of belief. One of the most spectacular buildings built in the first decades of Roman rule was the Temple of Claudius in Colchester. This building, with its marble covered portico, flanking altars and courtyard with a monumental entrance would have dominated the new *colonia* of Camulodunum. For both the retired veterans settled in the town and the native British tribes people in the surrounding area it was a very real reminder of the changing political and social order. The deification of the Emperor Claudius, despite his misgivings, gave a religious aura to the imperial throne. It also allowed the emperor to transcend the limitations of the human body. Wherever there was an altar, a shrine or temple to the Imperial cult, the deified emperor was immanent. This network of cult sites dedicated to the emperor attempted to create a web of religious worship across the Empire. Whether sacrifices being carried out in the emperor's name took place on Hadrian's Wall or in the deserts of Syria, they were focused on reminding the worshippers of the ever-present nature of Emperor and Empire. However, this web whilst wide was exceedingly thin. When Boudicca and her army sacked Colchester during her violent revolt against Roman rule the temple was destroyed.

Despite the widespread nature of the Imperial cult its followers seem to have been limited. Although it would have been the centre of periodic celebrations, these are likely to have been great public events carried out by the army or the civic government. For most of the inhabitants of Roman Britain such rituals would have had little impact. Instead, the archaeological remains of altars and other religious artefacts shows us that the people of Britain worshipped a wide range of gods and goddesses. There seems to have been no sense that people were limited to worshipping one deity, and most people probably had an extensive portfolio of religious loyalties, combining minor local spirits, possibly tribal gods and a certain attachment to some of the 'big hitters', whether in their British or Roman guise.

Five hundred years later, Roman political control of Britain was over. Although, many aspects of Roman rule had long faded, their influence was strong in other areas, and no more so than in religion. However, it was not a sentimental loyalty to Dea Romana or Jupiter that helped maintain a lively and productive literary culture or encouraged continual links with some of the most powerful men of Gaul. Instead it was loyalty to a new religion, Christianity, that served to bind together the splintered successor states of the Roman Empire and laid the foundation of medieval Europe. Unlike Islam, the other great new religion of the first millennium, Christianity was not initially spread by invasion and conquest. This book aims to explore the early stages of the equally profound, and no less spectacular, processes that led to the creation of Britain as a Christian country.

Early medieval views of Roman Christianity

The arrival of Christianity in Britain has been a subject of scholarly interest and historic consideration for well over 1,000 years. Although, even today, many people think that Christianity was brought to Britain by St Augustine in AD 597, early medieval writers were under no such illusion. The first historical, rather than strictly contemporary, record of the advent of the Church into Britain comes in the text known as the *De Excidio Brittonum* 'The Ruin of Britain'. This work is believed to have been written by a British monk named Gildas. Whilst its precise date is still a subject of debate, most scholars place it in the first half of the sixth century AD. The place of authorship is equally, if not more, debatable, with locations varying from the north-west of England to Cornwall; the current consensus seems to place him in south-west Britain, possibly Dorset, Gloucestershire or Somerset. Gildas was a member of the British church, which as we shall see, had the Christian Church in Roman Britain as its direct ancestor. Gildas himself has no doubts as to the origin of Christianity in Britain. He records his understanding of the situation in the early chapters of *De Excidio*. Although this work is frequently called a 'history', to see it as a straight chronicle of events in late Roman and early medieval Britain is to misunderstand its purpose. Whilst Gildas certainly outlined the historical developments of this period it was for a higher purpose. The heart of the book is an excoriation of the kings of Britain for failing in their Christian duty. As was typical of the early medieval period Gildas directly related the ebb and flow of the fortunes of their people to the moral probity of their leaders. Their military and political fortunes were seen as a clear barometer of their success in living up to the demands of Christian kingship. Gildas' purpose in chronicling the early years of the Church in Britain was to demonstrate this supposition. By relating the past fortunes and misfortunes of Britain and linking these to the state of the Church, Gildas aimed to substantiate and backup his diatribes against Britain's contemporary leaders. He was writing history with a purpose. It was not a disinterested record of events, but a powerfully subjective recounting of past events, shaped to help bolster modern moral messages.

According to Gildas 'Christ made a present of his rays' in the last years of the Emperor Tiberius (AD 14-37) (*De Excidio* 9). He seemed to think that Tiberius himself was Christian, and was in opposition to a pagan senate. He follows this with a record of the persecutions under Diocletian (see chapter 2), and records Britain's martyrs. The Church was restored after these purges and went through a golden period, when 'all her sons exulted, as though warmed in the bosom of the mother church' (*De Excidio* 12.2). Gildas then describes how the British church was split when the Arian heresy 'vomited its foreign poison'.

This outline appears completely at variance to what we now know about the history of the church in Britain from other sources. Whilst it is possible, if exceptionally unlikely, that some Christians may have lived in Britain as early as the reign of Tiberius, it is clearly preposterous to suggest that the Emperor himself was Christian or sanctioned its spread. Again, whilst it is possible that Arianism reached Britain there is no reason to believe it tore the British Church apart. Gildas' grasp of historical detail is equally tenuous in other areas; for example he placed the construction of Hadrian's Wall in the early fifth century. However, in some places Gildas' descriptions appear to faintly echo, if in a distorted manner, elements of the story of Christianity in the Roman Empire. For example, whilst a Christian Tiberius may never have been pitted against a pagan senate, later Christian emperors were forced to confront an entrenched and conservatively pagan senate, particularly in the second half of the fourth century AD. Equally, his description of the onslaught of Arianism may be a garbled version of the Pelagian controversy, which certainly did affect Britain. More importantly, however mistaken his understanding of history may be, it is clear that in the mid-sixth century the native British Christians were unequivocal that their Church was a direct ancestor of the Romano-British one and not a post-Roman implant.

Gildas was not the only early historian to record the arrival of Christianity to Roman Britain. The great Anglo-Saxon chronicler, Bede, writing in AD 731 recorded a different version in his *Ecclesiastical History of the English People*. He wrote that in AD 167 a certain British king named Lucius wrote to Pope Eleutherius (*c.*174-89) asking to be made Christian. Although some of Bede's information about Christianity in Britain, such as the arrival of Arianism, was clearly derived from Gildas, this story had another source. It is most likely to be a confused record of a similar appeal to the pope by a different Lucius. He was Prince of Edessa, in Syria which was known at the time as *Birtha* or *Britio Edessenorum*. The similarity in the names being the cause of this misunderstanding. The story of Lucius was probably derived from a copy of the *Liber Pontificalis*, a collection of biographies of early popes, which was known in England by the seventh century. Bede also included a more detailed record of the martyrdom of St Alban. Unlike Gildas he also records the Pelagian dispute, and notes the British origin of Pelagius himself.

Like Gildas, Bede was also writing with a distinct agenda; in this case, emphasising the political importance of his native kingdom of Northumbria, and belittling the native British Church at the expense of the strain of Christianity introduced by St Augustine, which had closer links with Rome. This may explain why Bede mentions Pelagianism, where Gildas did not. He was keen to paint the British Church as dangerously heterodox, with a propensity for heresy, in contrast to the firmly orthodox Anglo-Saxon Church.

Another important early historical source was the early ninth-century *Historia Brittonum*. The authorship of this work is conventionally ascribed to a British monk named Nennius, though the earliest versions do not include the preface in which he claims to be the writer. It is a curious text. The author claims 'I have made a heap of all that I have found'. It is certainly appears to be hotch-potch, containing an early history of Britain, a life of St Germanus, elements of chronicles recording the early history of Kent, a list of battles fought by King Arthur, royal genealogies and a list of the wonders of Britain. The extent to which this really is a random miscellany or a more carefully contrived collection is unclear, but if Bede was a supporter of the Anglo-Saxon Church, then Nennius was on the side of the British. However, he took Bede's story of Lucius, rather than following Gildas, suggesting that the Anglo-Saxon version of *Church history* in Britain was by now the prevailing orthodoxy.

Later medieval histories continued to record the Roman origins of the British Church. However, the further away in time they were, the more garbled and fanciful their narratives became. Geoffrey of Monmouth (*c*.1100–1150) repeated the story of Lucius, but also named two of the missionaries, Faganus and Duvianus, who were meant to have been sent to Britain. He also promoted the story that Helen, mother of the Emperor Constantine, was the daughter of King Coel ('Old King Cole'), a mythical ruler of the city of Colchester. The story of Joseph of Arimathea's arrival in Glastonbury first appeared in the *Deeds of the Kings of England* by William of Malmesbury (*c*.1095-1140). As well as these formalised narratives popular folklore also developed more confusing notions of the truth. For example, in York it was believed that Helen was actually buried on the site of the medieval church of St Helen-on-the-Walls. Intriguingly though, when the site was excavated the church was found to have been built over a Roman mosaic (**1**).

1 *The foundations of the medieval church of St Helen-on-the-Walls, traditionally the burial place of Helen, mother of the Emperor Constantine.* Copyright York Archaeological Trust

The growth of early Christian archaeology in Britain

A revived interest in the early history of Christianity in Britain took place in the sixteenth and seventeenth centuries. This renewed exploration of the theme took place against the religious controversies of the time, with the conflicts between the Catholic and Protestant Churches. The first historian to make a serious criticism of the traditions recounted by Geoffrey of Monmouth was the Italian historian Polydore Vergil (*c*.1470–*c*.1555). He was sent to England in 1501 as a collector of papal dues, where he became a friend of Henry VIII. He wrote a history of England, *Historiae Anglicae*, which carried these attacks on Geoffrey, noting 'Trulie ther is nothinge more obscure, more uncertaine, or unknowne then the affaires of the Brittons from the beginninge.' Although this provoked an angry response from Welsh writers such as John Price of Brecon it allowed the study of the Christian origins of Britain to begin on a more scholarly basis.

Following the transition of the English Church from Catholicism to Protestantism in the sixteenth century the study of the earliest of Christianity became of central importance. Just as for Bede and Gildas, seventeenth-century historians wanted to justify their religious beliefs through the medium of history. Protestant apologists wanted to show that their version of Christianity was not a radical reinterpretation of Christianity, but in fact its most authentic expression, arguing that Catholicism was in fact a misguided aberration. They did not take a uniform approach to these defences of their belief. One approach accepted that Christianity was introduced into Britain via the city of Rome, but argued that the way Christianity was practiced in Rome was fundamentally different from the later Roman Catholic faith which they believed had accreted theological errors. For other writers the very idea that British Christianity had ever had anything to do with the city of Rome smacked of popishness and instead they sought an earlier origin to the religion in Britain, showing how the links that brought it were directly from the Holy Land itself, and were thus never distorted by Rome.

Catholic writers also took two incompatible lines of defence. Some argued that Roman Christianity had died out early and the true heritage of the Church in England was that promoted by Bede, via Augustine and Pope Gregory. This view was promoted in Richard Verstegan's *A Restitution of decayed Intelligence in Antiquities* written in 1631. This important work was one of the first books to try and revive interest in Britain's Anglo-Saxon heritage, and contained the first published glossary of Old English words. Others accepted the success of earlier Christianity, and believed that this early Church was fundamentally Catholic in nature.

Whilst Catholic and Protestant Church historians could find very little to agree on, unwittingly they shared one point on which there was no dispute: the belief that the Church (however this might be understood) was a 'good thing'. With the rise of rationalist thought and the Enlightenment in the eighteenth century, the entire notion that Christianity was necessarily something that had a benign influence was challenged. Social thinkers began to challenge the authority of the Church to control debates about many aspects of knowledge, whether science, art, nature or history. For the first time since the time of the fifth-century pagan writers, it was questioned whether the rise of Christianity was inevitable, good or right. This viewpoint found its most ardent and eloquent proponent in Edward Gibbon. His mammoth work, the *Decline and Fall of the Roman Empire,* had one clear villain, the Christian Church. For Gibbon the clean moral lines of the Roman republic were made fuzzy by the advent of the institution of the Emperor and entirely swept away by the emergence of the Christian Church – the classical simplicity of Republican Rome was smothered by the baroque decadence of the Late Antique world.

Until the sixteenth century the study of Britain's past had remained primarily a historical rather than an archaeological subject. The focus was on the reinterpretation of the limited number of known texts, rather than the search for new data. However, from the seventeenth century, there was an increasingly antiquarian slant to the subject. Men such as William Camden and William Leland realised that any proper study of the past demanded the recording of physical remains. Whilst these early antiquarians considered the issue of early Christianity (Camden believed that the monotheism taught by the Druids presaged Christianity), they were hampered by the lack of archaeological objects.

In the early eighteenth century there was an increase in the number of archaeological remains being discovered. These included relics of all periods, from prehistory to medieval, but it was now that the first remains of a clearly Roman and Christian nature began to see the light of day. The first two objects, although found a long distance apart, were both pieces of precious silver plate. In Risley (Derbys.) a large rectangular silver plate of a type known as a *lanx* had been found by a ploughman in 1729. Although it was badly broken he kept the pieces. The antiquary William Stukely heard of the discovery and made a record of it. The object carried a clear *chi-rho* scratched on the base along with an inscription identifying it as possibly belonging to a Bishop 'of Bogiensis' (**2**). Although Stukely recognised the piece as Christian he did not feel comfortable viewing it as coming from Britain. Instead he believed it was captured as booty during fighting by the English near the town of Bouges in France in 1421.

2 *The Risely Park Lanx found in 1729*

Another silver vessel was found floating in the River Tyne close to the Roman fort and settlement of Corbridge. This was a small bowl, one of a number of pieces of silver plate to have been found in or near the river between the years 1736 and 1760. It was decorated with a series of six *chi-rho* symbols. A large silver *lanx* was also found in the same group of objects. At the time, the bowl and *lanx* were believed to be a chalice and a paten, and were thought to be part of a set of church plates. Another vessel from this group came from the Tyne near Bywell, and may have been washed from the bank. It bore the inscription: DESIDERI VIVAS ('long life to Desiderius'), which may also have Christian symbolism, though this was not recognised until the twentieth century.

At the other end of the country, and made of a lead rather than silver, another Christian vessel or container was found. This was the first of three lead tanks to be found in Icklingham (Suffolk) since the early eighteenth century. The circumstances of its discovery were described in 1728:

> About three years ago a Leaden Cistern was found here by a Ploughman, the Share striking against the Edge of it. The Treasure it had conceal'd was gone. The Cistern is in being; it contains about 16 Gallons, perforated on each Side for Rings to lift it by. There is ornamental Work on the Outside of it, imitating Hoops of Iron, but cast with the Thing it self. On one Side is a Mark A, perhaps intending the Measure or Use of it.

Like the dish from Bywell this tank was not recognised as being Christian until the twentieth century, when enough other examples bearing clear Christian images and symbols were found to allow a better understanding of this early discovery (**3**).

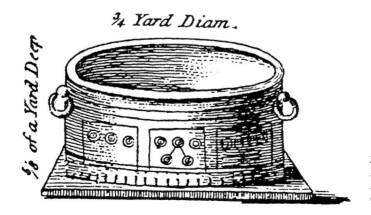

3 *Lead tank found in Icklingham in 1725. Illustrated in William Camden's* Britannia

In some cases the Christian identity of an object was recognised, though its Roman date was not. In the 1850s, an Anglo-Saxon cemetery site at Long Wittenham (Oxon.) was excavated by J.Y. Akerman. Amongst the other burials was the grave of a child containing a wooden beaker covered by a sheet of thin bronze with repoussée decorations. These showed three biblical scenes and a cross flanked by an alpha, and probably an omega. This was long thought to be of north Gaulish origin and of early medieval date. However, it is only recently that Martin Henig has argued that the object is almost certainly of Romano-British date and origin. It had presumably come into the possession of the family of the child sometime in the fifth century, and may well have been produced for a possible Christian community in nearby Dorchester-on-Thames in the fourth century.

The challenge of recognising church structures (which is explored fully in chapter 3) also meant that there was often confusion over the identification of early Christian buildings. The probable Christian nature of several buildings was not recognised at first. The church from Silchester was first excavated in 1892 by the Society of Antiquaries. The possible identification of the apsidal structure within the fort at Housesteads was not made when Robert Carr Bosanquet first excavated it in 1898. Conversely, a Roman building from the civilian settlement outside the Roman fort at Binchester (Co. Durham) was published in 1881 as a probable Christian meeting house. However, in the light of what we know today it is highly unlikely to be a church.

Despite these eighteenth- and nineteenth-century discoveries it was only in the twentieth century that a significant number of clearly Christian discoveries began to be made. A series of important hoards of precious metal objects were found. The earliest was found by archaeologists in 1919 at the Scottish hillfort of Traprain Law (E. Lothian). Several of the vessels carried religious symbols or depicted biblical scenes. Although found outside the area of Roman occupation these objects are most likely to have come via Britain, rather than arriving directly from abroad. Another important hoard was found in Mildenhall (Suffolk), this time not uncovered by archaeologists but by a ploughman. A second lucky ploughman found the Water Newton (Camb.) hoard in 1975. Many of the objects from both these hoards carried Christian symbols or inscriptions.

As well as these hoards, a number of excavations on Roman villas began to produce possible Christian decorative schemes. In 1963 a landowner discovered traces of a mosaic during preparation for building work on a field at Hinton St Mary, Dorset. Subsequent excavations revealed a large Christian mosaic. Not long previously excavations by Col. G.W. Meates in Kent found the fragmentary remains of the painted plasterwork from the walls of a small villa church. More churches also began to be recognised. Archaeological work beneath the medieval church of St Paul-in-the-Bail in the heart of the Lincoln found several earlier churches beneath it, the earliest being of Roman date.

Meanwhile in Colchester (Essex) excavations between 1976 and 1979 revealed not only a likely Christian cemetery at Butt Road, but also the remains of a church. Although traces of both had been discovered by the amateur archaeologist William Wire as early as the 1840s, their full extent and implication were only uncovered through this later excavation.

As well as these more spectacular discoveries of early Christian remains many other finds were made over the later nineteenth and twentieth centuries. Although some finds, such as a number of lead tanks continued to be found accidentally, an increasing number were being revealed in archaeological excavations. The more carefully controlled circumstances of their discovery allowed more precise dating, as this frequently relied on their position within the stratigraphy of the site.

Due to the increasing number of discoveries it was only in the second half of the twentieth century that scholars began to rise to the challenge of discussing the nature of Romano-British Christianity using archaeological as well as historical evidence. The earliest 'modern' attempt to synthesise the archaeological date for Christianity in Britain was a paper by the Francis Haverfield (1860-1919) written in 1896. However, it was published in the English Historical Review rather than an archaeological journal. It remained little known, and the topic of Christianity was barely mentioned by Haverfield in his seminal work *The Romanisation of Britain*.

The next major attempt was written by Jocelyn Toynbee in 1953. Toynbee was an art historian, and she laid the foundations for the study of Roman art in Britain. This was reflected in the way in which she approached the evidence of Romano-British Christianity. The focus of her paper was primarily in recognising Christian motifs or symbols on possible Christian objects. Such an approach was important, as the range of symbols used by early Christians and the problems these raised were perhaps not well known as it could have been in Britain. Her critical approach started to winnow the wheat from the chaff as far as archaeological evidence for Christianity in Britain was concerned. However, despite the increasing number of archaeological finds in the sixty years since Haverfield's article, their conclusions were similar, arguing for a church which had reached all ranks and was strongest in the Romanised southeast and south-west of England.

Since Toynbee's important paper a series of publications bringing together the archaeological evidence for Christianity have emerged. The most important of these is Charles Thomas' *Christianity in Roman Britain to AD 500* (1981), which brought together the historical, linguistic and archaeological evidence for Roman and sub-Roman Christianity in England, Wales and southern Scotland. Although over twenty years old, this book remains the first stop for anyone exploring the topic. However, inevitably important finds have been made since its publication, and there have been changes in approaches to the archaeological and historical sources. More recent attempts to gather together the information have included Dorothy Watts' *Christians and Pagans in Roman Britain* (1991) and Frances Mawer's *Evidence for Christianity in Roman Britain: The Small Finds* (1995).

Approaches to Romano-British Christianity

Although the study of Romano-British Christianity has inevitably been intimately linked with the growing body of archaeological evidence, approaches to the issue have varied enormously. Even today opinions about the state of Romano-British Christianity are widely divided. These modern opinions need to be situated within the history of the discipline and the context of the writers, as much as the work of Bede or Gildas does. One of the biggest divides in the subject has been between scholars who have approached the study of Roman Christianity in Britain from a background in early medieval or Celtic studies, and those with a background in Roman archaeology and history.

The interest by Celtic scholars in early Christianity grew partly from the increasing sense of regional and national identity in Scotland, Wales and Cornwall. One way in which these new political identities were expressed was through membership of the non-established churches, particularly Methodism and the Baptist Church. As local historians and antiquarians became increasingly aware of the distinct difference between the histories of England and its western peripheries there were attempts to link the past with present for semi-religious or political purposes.

The Church of England clearly traced its descent back to the mission of St Augustine who was sent by the Pope in AD 597. In the late nineteenth century it was becoming increasingly influenced by Catholic styles of worship under the Oxford Movement. For many the Church's historic link with Rome was worryingly tainted by papistry, and instead there was a search for other origin stories.

The increased realisation that many of the early medieval gravestones of Western Britain had parallels with similar stones from the Continent, and in particular southern Gaul opened new avenues of enquiry. Although relating to the Roman period such contacts need not have come via the Pope in Rome. It was known that there were very early communities of Christians in southern Gaul, many with links directly to the Holy Land. If it could be shown that when the Roman missionary Augustine arrived in England there was already a native British Church, which had its roots in Gaul and ultimately the eastern Mediterranean, then it was possible to make a case for the modern Churches in these areas as being both historically distinct and ultimately more orthodox. Even for those without such an interest in the niceties of *Church history* there was a general realisation that the religious trajectory of the west and north of Britain was distinctly different from that of the Anglo-Saxon areas.

This inevitably involved an exploration of its links with the Romano-British Church. *Christianity in Early Britain* by Hugh Williams was a crucially important book in this vein. Williams, a professor of *Church history* at the Theological College of Bala, carefully deconstructed many of the myths about the early Church, which frequently went back to Gildas, Bede and Geoffrey of Monmouth. He unravelled fact from fiction, and whilst outdated in places today, re-established the study of the early British (rather than Anglo-Saxon) Church as a serious historical field of enquiry, stripped from its accretions of legend and half-truths. Williams' believed that although there had been a Christian Church in Roman Britain, the worshippers belonged to the immigrant Roman communities rather than the native British communities, and that it did not survive the end of Roman rule. Instead he believed that the early medieval British Church had its roots in a Christian revival driven by monks from Southern Gaul. These non-conformist views contrasted with that of the new Catholic writers, such as Hilaire Belloc, who propagated views emphasising the failure of the Church in early medieval Britain, which had to be re-invigorated by the Augustinian mission, under the influence of which kingship and Christianity grew hand-in-hand.

Most recently, Charles Thomas, a native Cornishman, has followed the same path from early medieval Christianity to Romano-British Christianity. An extensive background in early medieval archaeology preceded his work on Romano-British Christianity, and *The Early Christian Archaeology of North Britain* (1971) is an important companion to *Christianity in Roman Britain*. In this book Thomas argued cogently that the Christian church in Roman Britain continued to thrive in the fifth century. He distinguished between a Roman or sub-Roman Church which lasted until the *c*.AD 500 and a post-Roman Church. For him, this divide was marked by the arrival of monasticism, first in south-west Britain and south Wales and then Ireland. He was clear that this transition affected a healthy Church, and was not a revival of a stagnant religion through contacts with a more vibrant continental Church. More importantly he saw the success of Christianity in Roman Britain not just as an interesting but ultimately unimportant aspect of fourth- to sixth-century culture in Britain. Instead, he argued: 'if Continuity (of the British Romans, their life and languages, and of Britannia) is the horse that draws this vehicle into the fifth century, the Church is the rider.' Thomas' views, however, were not supported by the important early medieval scholar, Ralegh Radford, another archaeologist with West Country origins. In a study of the early Christian origins of Britain he wrote: 'It shows that in this field at least Roman Britain made no significant contribution to the rise of the insular church in the fifth century'.

In the 'Roman' camp, one of the most significant scholars in the field has been William Frend. A former professor of Ecclesiastical History at the University of Glasgow, his work on early Christianity has ranged widely across the Roman world. He excavated early Christian sites in Algeria in the 1930s and worked at Qasr Ibrim (Egypt), where he was involved in the discovery of a collection of fourteenth-century Coptic scrolls. His work on early Christianity in Roman Britain has come in a series of articles, published since 1955. Despite his archaeological work, his views on Britain have been based primarily on the historical rather than the archaeological evidence. He has consistently argued that the Church was in terminal decline before the end of the fourth century. He has related this failure to both systemic failures and specific political events. The crux of his argument was that the Church was too reliant on the patronage of a section of the Romanised landowners and the urban organisation of the *civitates* to survive their downfall. He contrasted the situation in Britain with that of Gaul, and particularly noted that Britain lacked an equivalent of St Martin of Tours whose militant anti-paganism led to a concerted attack on non-Christian belief and practices in northern Gaul. This strengthened the power of the Gaulish Church in the late fourth century, a period of real political and social crisis. He placed the death of the Roman Church in Britain in the 360s, when it was weakened not only by the pagan revival under the Emperor Julian, but more importantly the so-called 'Barbarian Conspiracy' of 367-9, a crisis that occurred only in Britain, and not in Gaul or Spain. Frend connected this failure of the Church with the wider failure of Roman control in Britain to last beyond the early fifth century, with the episcopal organisation of the Church finally disappearing by the mid-fifth century. Britain failed to deal with the problems caused by increased raiding and migration from Scotland, Ireland and mainland Europe because the Church had not survived to exert a unifying force in the face of these invasions, unlike it had elsewhere in the Western Empire. Ultimately, there was a 'church, which though rich in personalities and ideas, lacked the popular support that ensured survival in the West'. Whilst he accepts that there was some continued Christianity in Britain into the fifth century he felt that 'the *ecclesia Britannorum* failed to provide the foundations for the *ecclesia Anglicana*'.

The notion that the Romano-British Church failed in the second half of the fourth century has more recently been supported by Dorothy Watts in *Religion in Late Roman Britain* (1998). Drawing on the evidence for Christianity she had laid out in an earlier book she put forward the hypothesis that Britain underwent a major revival of paganism in the period 360-391 which stunted the growth of the Church. Like Frend she identified structural weaknesses in the British Church, including the failure of a parochial system to develop as well as a certain 'paganisation' of Christian practice. Combined with an economic failure in the later fourth century and the hammer blow of the end of Roman political control, this meant that Christianity in the end was unable to defeat native British paganism.

Despite these studies, until recently Romano-British Christianity has not been dealt with critically by archaeologists writing more general historical and archaeological syntheses of Roman Britain. Haverfield barely mentioned it in the *Romanisation of Britain* or the *Roman Occupation of Britain*, beyond observing that it had spread widely, except in the army. In his seminal work *Britannia* Sheppard Frere reflected on the irony that 'at the moment that Britain ceased to be part of the Roman Empire she was becoming united as never before with the state religion of the Roman Empire'.

Haverfield, Collingwood and Frere all considered the end of Roman Britain. In the twentieth century there have been a range of differing interpretations of the effects of Roman withdrawal. In the 1930s Collingwood believed that there were some elements of continuity in Roman life into the fifth century, with Roman Britain ending with the death of Arthur in the late fifth century. He did not deny a decrease in settlement occupation in fifth-century Britain, but he described this as a peaceful desertion rather than the result of violence. He saw the end of Roman Britain, not in terms of a conflict of peoples, but a conflict of traditions: Germanic versus Romano-British. This conflict was complicated by a 'backwash of Celticism'. J.N.L. Myres also considered the end of Roman Britain in depth. He saw the fifth century as a period of disintegration for the Romano-British, with town life and villa life declining. Nonetheless, he did not see the integration of British and Germanic society as occurring until the early to mid-sixth century. Although both Collingwood and Myres saw the Saxon settlements as spelling the end of Roman Britain it was a slow drawn-out death; the withdrawal of troops in AD 407 was an important event, but it was symptomatic of a more long-term change in Roman Britain. Sheppard Frere placed the end of Roman Britain yet earlier. He emphasised the important effect that the cessation of the Roman coin supply had on the economy of fifth-century Britain, leading to a collapse of local industries and a return to a more barter-based economy. He accepts, though, that the early years of the fifth century were a period of prosperity, which was ended by the revolt of the Saxon *foederati* in AD 442. It was at this point that he saw the end of Roman Britain: 'thereafter it was Celtic rather than Roman Britain which maintained the struggle'. None of these authors saw the success or otherwise of Roman Christianity as having any wider influence on the events of the fifth century.

This lack of emphasis on the wider social and political role of Romano-British Christianity is also found in more theoretical and analytical studies of the end of Roman Britain. Although his book *The Romanisation of Britain* is a detailed study of the processes of culture change in Roman Britain, Martin Millett does not address the role of the Church at all. In an earlier exploration of cultural change in Somerset in the Roman to early medieval period in Somerset, Philip Rahtz grudgingly accepted that Christianity may have provided a unifying ideology in a time of stress, but was very pessimistic about any evidence for the success and spread of Christianity in the fourth and fifth centuries. Importantly, both these studies were exercises in archaeological rather than historical analysis. Rahtz drew on models of system collapse developed by Colin Renfrew whilst studying the prehistoric East Mediterranean and Millett's work used anthropological and socio-economic models. Millett did, however, note that the historical and archaeological evidence for the end of Roman Britain were contrasting, and pointed out that the historical evidence was not a product of the socio-economic system, which was his primary focus of study. By exploring the end of Roman Britain in terms of structural socio-economic terms rather than in political terms both these analyses sidelined Christianity and the wider role of religion.

In the last fifteen years there has been a significant increase in the study of the late Roman to early medieval transition, with important books by Simon Esmonde Cleary, Ken Dark, Neil Faulkner, Nicholas Higham and Michael Jones amongst others. These reflect a wider, long-term, increasing interest in the study of the late Roman period across the Roman Empire. The study of Late Antiquity (the period from *c.*AD 200-700) has emphasised the central role that Christianity took in recasting the culture and civilisation of the Classical world. It has shown that religious change was not a mere sideshow, but a process that fundamentally changed the world-view of the inhabitants and neighbours of the Roman Empire. The notion of Late Antiquity has traditionally not been used by scholars studying this period in Britain; instead the period division has been drawn squarely at the end of Roman rule in 410. However, these new studies have started to take this period as a field of study in its own right. For example in a study of Roman art in Britain, Martin Henig has argued that late Roman art in Britain should be seen as part of a broader continuum of Late Antique art, and compared with the artistic output of the rest of the Late Antique world. Whilst views may differ wildly about the events in this complex period there is now an agreement that transition from 'Roman' Britain to early medieval Britain is a significant field of study in its own right, and not a topic that can be tacked onto the end of books on Roman Britain or the beginning of books on medieval Britain.

We have already seen that Charles Thomas closely linked the success of the Church with a high level of continuity from Roman Britain. Conversely Frend linked what he perceived as the catastrophic collapse of Roman society in Britain with what he believed was the failure of the Church. This connection of the state of the Church with the nature of the post-Roman transition is not a new one. Perhaps the most notable early attempts to relate the two have concerned the nature of the Pelagian heresy (discussed more fully in chapter 2). This heresy, which we have historical evidence for in Britain from the mid-fifth century, has been seen as having political overtones as well as religious implications.

The noted Anglo-Saxon scholar J.N.L. Myres first brought Pelagianism to a central position in the events of the early fifth century. He argued that the heresy was most widespread amongst wealthy landowners. He believed that these men came to dominate the early to mid-fifth-century ruling group of Britain, including such figures as Vortigern. Myres suggested that a combination of a revolt by his Anglo-Saxon mercenaries and a concerted attack on Pelagianism from the Gaulish Church led to Vortigern's downfall. John Morris, in a slightly later paper, advocated a more politically radical Pelagianism, which precipitated the replacement of a British successor government with a Pelagian-influenced government, which supporters of the heresy urged to implement egalitarian policies. Both these models have attracted a great deal of criticism, particularly for imputing a political edge to the movement which many believe it never had. However, the importance of these hypotheses lies in the fact that the authors were prepared to give the Church a central and powerful role in the political developments of the fifth century.

More recently Ken Dark has also argued for a more central role of the Church at this time. In *Civitas to Kingdom* he challenges the idea of a late fourth-century pagan revival. He suggested that by the end of the fourth century there was widespread, rural, lower-status Christianity and a high-status paganism, arguing that this reflected wider social tensions between landowners and their tenants. Moving into the fifth century, he linked a general empire-wide increase in Christian militancy with social upheaval along the lines of the Gaulish peasant revolt known as the *bacaudae*. In a more recent book he has emphasised the continuity of a 'Roman-Christian' culture in Britain into the sixth century with a fundamental transformation only occurring in the seventh century. In direct opposition, Neil Faulkner, who argues that Roman Britain underwent a short, sharp collapse, believes that Christianity was neither widespread nor deep-rooted. In contrast to Dark he believes that it was an exclusive, upper class religion. He follows others in suggesting a peasant revolt, influenced by the *bacaudae*, but gives it no religious subtext.

A final, and more unusual, interpretation put forward for the role of the religion comes from Dominic Perring. Again, he argues that it was a preserve of the elites, but importantly he has suggested that rather than following orthodox beliefs these worshippers instead opted for a more arcane and esoteric version, commonly called Gnosticism. These beliefs focused around initiation rituals and the transmission of knowledge leading to salvation, with little emphasis on traditional congregational worship. He sees Gnosticism as being attractive to the British elite because the failure of cities to thrive in the fourth century led to a weak town-based episcopal Church, with power being exercised by these elites from their rural villas. The failure of the Church encouraged this rarefied retreat into an eclectic but exclusive brand of Christianity.

Clearly, Christianity potentially has a central role in exploring the nature of late Roman and early medieval Britain. The scholars discussed above have raised important questions about the status of the Church. How widespread was it? Who were its members? Did it survive into the fifth century? The answers to these questions have important implications for the wider study of late Roman Britain.

Until now we have been exploring the developing ideas archaeologists and historians have had about the nature of Christianity in Roman Britain. However, it is important to explore the way in which people have reached their opinions. Historical texts may clearly have their biases, which can be taken account of when analysing them. But how far is this true of the archaeological remains of worship? In many traditional accounts the physical evidence for Christianity is taken as an uncomplicated reflection of the spread of the religion. The unspoken assumption is that the heart and soul of Christianity exists in its writings.

The Bible was certainly the central plank of Christian belief, though as we shall see in chapter 2, it was only coalescing into its final form in the late fourth century. Around the Bible were the many writings of the early church fathers, expanding on points of theology, defending Christianity from attacks against first pagans and later heretics, and searching for a deeper understanding of the Bible itself. However, this vast outpouring of religious writing has understandably dominated the way in which many scholars have explored Christianity. This preoccupation with the written word has led to the sidelining of the archaeological evidence. Whilst it has frequently been used to illustrate the spread of Christianity it is rare that archaeology is used to explore differences and variation in Christian religious belief. It is important to remember though, that despite Christianity's reputation for being essentially a 'religion of the word' the majority of Christian worshippers, particularly in a province such as Britain, would have been illiterate. They were unable to read the Bible, and could not follow the increasingly rarefied theological debates of the fourth and fifth centuries. For most, their knowledge of their religion would have come from participating in religious ceremonies. Obviously, these would have included listening to the Bible being read aloud, but they would also be surrounded by the physical dimensions of the church – they would sit in churches decorated with wall paintings, celebrate the Eucharist using vessels decorated with biblical scenes and be baptised in fonts decorated with religious symbols. Although a few British Christians, such as Patrick or Pelagius, were able to express and communicate their beliefs in writing, this option would not have been open to most. Instead, they were able to carve religious symbols or contribute towards expensive gifts to the church. Even those who were able to read and write had other avenues open to them when expressing their religious views; a letter may be read by perhaps a dozen people, but a mosaic or a painted wall would be seen by many more. If we want to know about the finer points of theology, then we must certainly turn to historical evidence, but if we want to know about what religion actually meant to most worshippers we must deal with the archaeological remains.

Because of the central role which buildings, objects and arts took in Christianity it is important to analyse it carefully. People use powerful and holy images thoughtfully, and think about the places in which they do, or do not, use them. The location in which religious objects were used or disposed of is very important. However, there were also constraints over what people could do; worshippers were limited by their economic wealth, social propriety or their pre-existing ideas about religion. This means that the distribution of archaeological remains is a complex one. However, earlier authors have not always dealt with this complexity.

Most studies of Christianity in Britain have focused on the basic procedure of identifying Christian objects. Following this approach, the study of the spread of the religion in Britain should be fairly simple. The presence or absence of diagnostic Christian or pagan archaeological objects should be able to be used to plot the introduction and growth of Christianity. However, it is not always easy to identify Christian objects or symbols. As this present study and other books have shown some objects are clearly Christian, but with other artefacts or buildings it is less clear. This has led to attempts to add a 'weighting' or 'scoring' systems. Clearly Christian sites such as the wall paintings from Lullingstone achieve a high score, whilst more dubious finds get a lower score. Whilst the range and reliability of various criteria have been debated the basic concept that there is a discrete set of Christian ritual practices that are recognisable in the archaeological record has rarely been challenged. Following this approach, the study of the process of religion in Roman Britain should be fairly simple. The presence or absence of diagnostic Christian or pagan archaeological markers should be able to be used quantitatively to plot the introduction and growth of Christianity.

It is this broad approach which has been used in the two most recent discussions of the subject: Charles Thomas' *Christianity in Roman Britain to AD 500* and Dorothy Watts' *Christians and Pagans in Roman Britain*. Both books use systems of relative weighting. Having identified varying numbers of Christian artefacts and sites, both go on to create maps of the level of Christianity in late Roman Britain (**4**). However, in both cases it is not entirely clear what these maps are intended to represent. Although in reality they are condensed maps of a range of different types of objects, from possible church structures to pottery with *chi-rho* symbols, there is an assumption that this can be simply converted to an actual relative level of Christianity. Quite what this 'relative density' means, is never really made clear – does it indicate a higher relative proportion of practising Christians in a community, or a higher absolute level, or just varying degrees of fervency amongst believers? As we shall see later, the distribution of different objects varies quite considerably. Christian lead tanks are found in different locations to villas with Christian remains. Possible Christian gravestones are found in yet another area. However, these variations are lost in such maps.

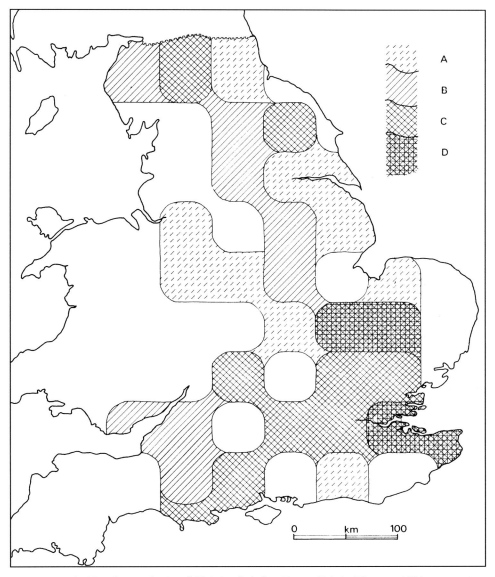

4 *Map showing density of Christian finds from Roman Britain.* Thomas, 1981

They give a spuriously objective image idea of the spread of the religion, but in their attempts to be quantitative they lose a lot of qualitative information. By unteasing these maps it is possible to create a more textured map of Christianity in Roman Britain.

As well as looking at the wider geographical context of objects it is also important to consider the type of sites in which they are found. For example, why is Christian imagery so common on late Roman belt sets, but not on brooches, hair pins or other such adornments? It is not enough to point out that lead tanks decorated with Christian symbols are mainly found in the east of England. We must ask why they are so often found in wells, marshes, rivers and other watery sites. This book attempts to examine the archaeology of Roman Christianity by exploring the remains at this level of data. Rather than lumping information together I have tried to uncover these variations and differences. Hopefully, it will give us a better understanding of the earliest Christians in Britain.

2

HISTORICAL BACKGROUND

When Christianity first arrived in Britain is unclear. Like most Roman provinces there would have been a constant flow of incomers from abroad, both from Rome itself and its many territories. Tombstones from Britain record the burials of individuals from Gaul, Spain, Greece and even as far as Palmyra, a caravan city in what is now Syria. It is certainly possible that some of these visitors may have been practising Christians. However, there is a huge difference between the presence of transient worshippers and the establishment of permanent communities. The earliest evidence for Christian worship in Britain was once thought to be a word-square scratched onto a small fragment of an amphora found in a late second-century pit in the civilian settlement outside the fort at Manchester (**5**). The inscriptions reads: ROTAS / OPERA / TEN [ET / AREPO / SATOR], meaning 'Arepo, the sower, holds the wheels carefully'. These words can be rearranged to form a cross-shaped word pattern showing the words PATER NOSTER ('Our father'), and the letters A and O, representing the Greek letters alpha and omega.

```
                              A

                              P
                              A
                              T
                              E
                              R
              A  P A T E R N O S T E R  O
                              O
                              S
                              T
                              E
                              R

                              O
```

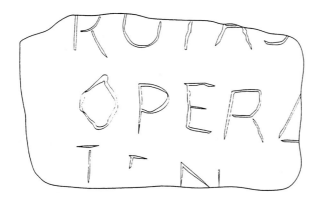

5 *Word-square from Manchester scratched onto a fragment of amphora.* Drawing by Mike Bishop from Mawer, 1995

Another similar word-square has also been found written on a fragment of wall plaster from Cirencester. This has also been dated to around the second or third century AD. However, the Christian interpretation of these word-squares has been questioned. Several are known from Pompeii, which was destroyed in AD 79, which is early for widespread use of even such cryptic Christograms. It has also been pointed out that the phrase PATER NOSTER was not used as a particularly Christian term until the sixth century AD or later. Equally important, the simple cross was not used as a Christian symbol until the fourth or fifth centuries AD, certainly not in the second or third. It is most likely that although these squares had religious symbolism, it was not necessarily Christian; Mithraic connections have also been put forward, and many pagan religions, particularly those with Eastern influences, had an interest in numerology.

The first references to the presence of a more established Church, like so much of the written evidence for Christianity in Britain, comes from foreign writers. Around AD 200 Tertullian, a North African writer, wrote in his book *Adversus Judaeos* (Against the Jews) of '. . . the haunts of the Britons – inaccessible to the Romans, but subjugated to Christ . . .' (*Ad Jud* 7). This was part of a list of other places in the Empire, which had been converted to Christianity. He included amongst these Persia, North Africa and the barbarian tribes of northern and eastern Europe. His near-contemporary, Origen, also wrote that the Church had reached the lands of Britain ('*terra Britanniae*') and the 'very end of the world'. However, it is necessary to exercise a certain caution when dealing with these declarations of the triumph of the Church. These works were written to glorify the success of a still illegal church, which continued to face active persecution at times. They have a strong rhetorical element, and these references to Britain and the edges of empire may have been similar to references to Timbuctu today. Despite this, it is possible that these writings originate from some reality. As it stands, these references suggest that for the audience and writer of these tracts it was felt that it was at least possible that Christianity had reached Britain and elsewhere. It would have been difficult for the early Christian writers to make completely spurious statements about the progress of the religion, and their preaching had to have at least a semblance of truth.

Christianity continued its slow but steady growth through the third century. The increased level of persecution of Christian communities in the mid-third century perhaps reflected its success. In AD 249-51 there was a phase of persecution under the Emperor Decius followed by a second period under Valerian between AD 257 and 259. Under Decius, people suspected of being Christian were forced to clear themselves of suspicion by making sacrifices to Roman gods, and then getting a certificate known as a *libellus*, which showed that they had made these sacrifices and were above any further suspicion.

It was during one of these phases of anti-Christian agitation that Britain's first known martyrs may have been executed. The sixth-century writer Gildas refers to the Aaron and Julius, citizens of Caerleon as martyrs who 'displayed the highest spirit in the battle-line of Christ' (*De Excidio* 10:2). The Roman fort at Caerleon, the headquarters of the II Augusta legion probably fell out of use in the late third century (*c*.AD 287-96). This means it is unlikely that the execution of these two martyrs took place in the persecutions of the early fourth century. Although Caerleon was a major military base, it is not certain that Aaron and Julius were soldiers as there was also a civilian settlement associated with the fort.

Following the pressure exerted on Christian communities in this period the Emperor Gallienus, the successor to Valerian, committed an abrupt *volte-face*. In AD 260 he issued an edict declaring that Christianity would now be tolerated as an accepted religion within the Empire. In the terms of the time it became a *religio licita*. This had important implications; as well as allowing the obvious freedom of worship it allowed the Church to hold property as a corporate body. Previously, most church property would have been held by individuals, which would have prevented the long-term growth of a secure economic basis for local churches and the development and investment in their properties. Gallienus' Edict was followed by a series of rescripts (private replies) to local communities of bishops. The Church historian Eusebius reproduced a rescript to Egyptian bishops in his *Church history* (*CH* 7:13). The significance of these rescripts is that it showed that the Roman administration, even at this early stage of the Church, recognised the role of bishops in representing the wider Christian community. The Egyptian rescript also stated that the bishops could reclaim the possession of the 'so-called cemeteries'. This may imply that at this stage, in Egypt at least, there were distinct Christian cemeteries, which may also have been the site of some forms of worship. How far this rescript dealing with Egypt reflects those that must have been written to the western Roman bishops is a different matter.

The third century was a period of general change in the Roman Empire, with political and economic upheavals. In the fifty years before Diocletian became emperor in AD 284 there were over twenty official emperors. In an attempt to impose some order on imperial succession Diocletian instituted the system known as the tetrarchy. This involved dividing the Empire into two divisions of command: Diocletian taking the East and Maximian the West. Each of these senior emperors then appointed a second who would succeed on the elder's retirement. Although the system did not last long it was a clear indication that the Empire was willing to experiment with new systems of government in order to ensure the stability that the previous years had lacked.

The political uncertainty had been compounded by increased economic problems. The main silver coins, the *denarius* and *antonianus,* were massively debased, ending up as a *de facto* bronze coinage. This in turn pushed out the pre-existing bronze coinage. Although the extent to which this caused or was caused by large-scale inflation is debated, it was certainly a symptom of increasing fiscal difficulties for the state. This would have been most apparent in the realm of state expenditure, of which payment of its armies was a significant element. These armies also saw great changes in the third and early fourth century, particularly under Constantine. The old army had been divided into two broad classes: the legions who were recruited from citizens of the Empire, and formed the backbone of the fighting force, and the auxiliaries who were made up of men who did not hold citizenship. They supplied the army's scouts, skirmisher, cavalry and light infantry. Although the army retained this dual structure, the division was now between the *limitatenses*, who were responsible for guarding boarders and frontier posts and the *comitatenses* who were a better trained mobile field army, intended to provide defence in depth. They were stationed away from the borders, and were usually based in or near towns or even billeted with civilians.

The changes in the army were also paralleled by changes in the civil administration of the Empire. The territorial divisions of the Empire were reformed. Britain, previously one province known as Britannia, was divided into four provinces: Britannia Prima, Britannia Secunda, Maxima Caesariensis and Flavia Caesariensis. These were governed by *praeses.* Together they made up the *diocese* of Britannia administered by a *vicarius* based in London. Below the level of the province were the cities or *civitates*. In Britain these roughly corresponded to the old Iron Age tribal territories. The administration of these was overseen by a *corrector*. He ensured the efficient running of the territories by the local *ordo*, a council made up by members of the local landowners. Although an honourable position in the earlier centuries, by the third century the financial responsibilities incurred by membership of the *ordo* made it increasingly burdensome, though it probably remained a privileged position.

Thus at the end of the third century the Empire had seen political instability with renewed attempts to finds solutions to this problem. There was a reformed army, with a new field army increasingly based within civilian areas, as well as the military zones. The reorganisation of the civil administration also saw an increase in provincial capitals with their associated civil service, bringing the officers of the imperial administration closer to the population. All this occurred against a background of financial difficulties. Given these changes it is not surprising there were perceptible shifts in the state's attitude to religion.

There are clear indications that although the final victory of Christianity was not inevitable there were wider shifts occurring in the religious sphere. There seemed to be a move both towards monotheism (the worship of only one god) and a reworking of the relationship between the Emperor and the gods. The deification of dead emperors was a tradition going back to at least the first century AD. However, the political anarchy of the third century with its multiplicity of emperors destabilised the power and gravitas of the imperial cult. Some emperors appear to have cast about for alternative ways of relating the office of emperor with a godhead. The best-known example of this was the attempt by Aurelian (AD 270-5) to promote the cult Sol Invictus. The other gods were subordinated to Sol, and Aurelian claimed to be a living divinity, an important move away from the deification only of dead emperors. There were also important changes under Diocletian. As part of his newly instituted tetrarchy he was equated with Jupiter and the other Augustus with Hercules, although they did not claim directly to be gods. This development saw the relationship of the post of emperor with a particular god, with an emphasis on the office rather than holder of the office. These two imperial experiments in theology show an attempt to create a new relationship between the Emperor and religion, and the ground was beginning to be laid for the later success of the Church.

Despite the apparent relaxation of attitudes to Christianity in the later third century following Gallienus' edict there was a sudden shift away from this easy attitude of toleration. In AD 303 Diocletian began a new persecution against Christians. This had been preceded by a purge of Christians in the army. The opening stages of this persecution included the destruction of the great church in Nicomedia in Asia Minor. This was followed by an edict authorising wider persecution. Christians holding public office were stripped of their rank, and in the east bishops were imprisoned. Under the tetrarchy it was up to the Augusti how they carried out the persecution, and it is thought that the persecution under Constantius in the west was lukewarm, and he is only recorded as demolishing a few churches. However, it is possible that it was during this persecution that Britain's best-known saint, Alban, was martyred. The story of St Alban's martyrdom is recorded in several early histories: Constantius' *Vita Germani*, Gildas' *De Excidio* and Bede's *Ecclesiastical History*. However, these all probably derived their information from an early retelling of the death of St

Alban, the *Passio Albani*. The oldest version of this text survives in Turin, and probably dates to the late eighth century. However, this is merely the first surviving version of an undoubtedly older text. It is possible to define more closely the date of the *Passio*. As it was used by Gildas, whose work is generally accepted to belong to the first half of the sixth century, it must have been written before this time. The *Passio* mentions a visit of St Germanus to the shrine of St Alban in AD 429, so it must have been committed to paper after this date. A recent study of the textual history of the *Passio* by Richard Sharpe has suggested that it was probably composed sometime between AD 430 and 480, and it may have been based on details of the saint's life painted onto wooden placards in Germanus' church in Auxerre.

According to the *Passio* and the retellings in Bede and Gildas, Alban was arrested for hiding a fugitive Christian from his persecutors and swapping clothes with him. Although these events are traditionally associated with the Roman town of *Verulamium* (St Albans) (**6**), the first writer to directly locate them there was Bede who was writing in the eighth century AD. In his new guise it was claimed that he performed several miracles including creating a new crossing over the channel of a river, leading over a thousand men across in an event with clear echoes of Moses' parting of the Red Sea. He was ultimately arrested and brought before a judge who ordered him to make sacri-

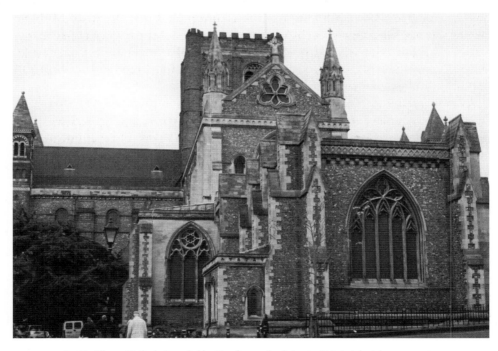

6 *St Albans Cathedral, probable site of an early shrine to Britain's best-known martyr*

fices to the gods. On Alban's refusal he was condemned to death. He was brought to an area outside the town where a large crowd had gathered. The executioner refused to carry out the judgement. Alban then ascended a hill, where a spring appeared at his feet. He was then beheaded. The executioner was immediately punished when his eyes dropped out. The first soldier who refused to carry out the execution was then also beheaded.

The precise date of this martyrdom is unclear. Gildas fails to give a date, though he conjectures that it took place during one of the main persecutions. Bede states that the events occurred during the rule of Diocletian (*EH* 6, 7). However, other possible dates have been put forward. The scholar John Morris seized upon the fact that the version of the *Passio* held in Turin stated that the judge was called Caesar. He suggested that this implied that the events must have taken place between AD 208 and 211 when the Emperor Severus was in Britain to conduct military campaigns in Scotland. He left his son, Geta, in charge as the governor of Britain. Geta had been given the official title *Caesar*, and it was on this basis that Morris suggested that Alban's death was ordered by Geta personally. However, it has since been shown that the passage referring to Caesar was probably a later addition to the text, inserted in the sixth or seventh century, and therefore cannot be used to date the events. Recently, Martin Henig has suggested that the events could have taken place under the rule of Constantius I after the end of the breakaway rule of the Carausius and Allectus. He has put forward the possibility that Alban had in fact sheltered a political refugee who was hiding from retribution, and that the story of these events was converted into a religious narrative. He also points out that many elements of the story of Alban's execution are redolent of themes from Celtic and Romano-British religious practices, with the implications that much, if not all, of the story may be entirely mythical.

As his tetrarchic system demanded, Diocletian retired in AD 305 and withdrew to his place in Split. However, the tetrarchy was soon to collapse. His brother emperor in the West Constantius died in AD 306 whilst campaigning in Britain. His son Constantine was raised to the position of Augustus by his troops in York on 25 July AD 306 (**7**). The events following his elevation are unclear. Although Constantine was the emperor who would make Christianity the state religion, it is not clear at this early stage that he was a believer. A panegyric written by an anonymous author in AD 307 equates Constantine with the name Hercules, the god whom his ally the former Augustus, Maximian, had adopted. A later panegyric of AD 310 claimed that he had seen a vision of Apollo, who was often equated with Sol Invictus, the sun god promoted in the late third century by Aurelian. Indeed, Sol Invictus soon replaced Mars on Constantine's coins.

On Diocletian's retirement the persecutions of Christians had not all ceased. Although in the West the persecutions, which had been minor under Constantius, probably faded away completely, in the East they continued under

Galerius, who only called them off on his deathbed. It is likely that Constantine had too many other issues on his plate. In AD 310 he had to deal with challenges from his former ally Maximian who had seized Rome, and his son Maxentius who turned on both his father and Constantine. Maximian committed suicide, but it took another two years before Constantine dealt with Maxentius, whom he defeated in a battle at the Milvian Bridge over the Tiber on 28 October AD 312. This left him in charge in the West, with Licinius who had succeeded Galerius as Augustus in the East.

Constantine was traditionally meant to have seen a vision of a cross of light in the weeks leading up to the battle. However, in Eusebius' first account of the victory in his *Church History* no references were made to any such event. It was only in his *Life of Constantine* written after Constantine's death that the story was related. A similar story, telling how Constantine had a dream in which he was told to ensure that his soldiers carried a *chi-rho* on their shields, was also told by Lactantius in *On the Deaths of the Persecutors* (c.AD 314). It is perhaps from this source that Eusebius developed his account. Constantine had earlier been attributed with having a vision of Apollo before his temporary interest in Sol Invictus. It is not unlikely that Constantine realised the political usefulness of having visions, and his vision or dream at Milvian Bridge may have less to do with blinding revelation and more to do with *realpolitik*.

Whatever the precise events before the battle, the aftermath is clearer. Licinius had to deal with threats to his own position from Maximin, the nephew of Galerius. However, he defeated him in AD 313. The two Augusti became closely allied, and shortly before his battle with Maximin, Licinius married Constantine's sister. The great breakthrough for Christianity finally came in the same year when the two emperors issued the so-called Edict of Milan, which allowed for religious toleration and effectively ended the persecution of Christianity in the Empire.

It was clear that having freed the Church, Constantine planned to take an active part in the conduct of church affairs. His first intervention was to attempt to solve the Donatist dispute. During the persecution of Christians under Diocletian and his successors, many Christians, particularly in North Africa, had 'lapsed' and temporarily given up their faith. However, with the end of the pressure on the church many of these wanted to return to the fold of the Church. The Church in general was happy to accept the return of these lost sheep, but the followers of Donatus took a much more hard-line position and would not support their readmission. Constantine's first attempt to deal with the dispute was by convening a council of bishops in Rome, but when its judgement went against them the Donatists refused to accept the result, claiming it was not representative. This led to Constantine calling a church council at Arles in AD 314. To ensure the widest possible acceptance of its judgements he made efforts to force as many bishops as possible to attend, and extended the use of the imperial post system to them. It is in the

7 *Modern statue of Constantine outside York Minster*

records of this council that we have the first unequivocal evidence of a Christian Church in Britain. In the proceedings of the council, the *Acta Concilii Arelatensis*, a number of bishops from Britain are mentioned. Although the reading of this list is slightly corrupt it reads:

> *Eborius episcopus de civitate Eboracensi provincia Brittania*
> *Restitutus episcopus de civitate Londiniensi provincia suprascripta*
> *Adelphius episcopus de civitate Colonia Londiniensium*
> *Exinde Sacerdos presbyter Arminius diaconus.*

The first bishop in the list, Eborius, came from York (*Eboracum*). The next, Restitutus, came from London, the capital of the late Roman diocese of Britain. These two identifications are quite clear. However, the location of *Colonia Londiniensium* is less clear, and both Colchester and Lincoln have been suggested, though the latter is more likely. The final line states that the party also included Sacerdos, a priest, and Arminius, a deacon. Interestingly, the three bishops appear to come from not merely Roman towns, but the capitals of three of the four provinces of Britain: London was the capital of Maxima Caesariensis, York was probably the capital of Flavia Caesariensis and Lincoln the capital of Britannia Secunda. This leaves one province, Britannia Prima, without a representative bishop. It is possible that for some reason this province may have been temporarily without a bishop, and that Arminius and Sacerdus represented its interests. The capital of Britannia Prima is most likely to have been Cirencester, as a governor is recorded on a dedication inscription from the town. It is unlikely that the representatives of the church from the four provinces were the only bishops in Britain. They were probably metropolitan bishops representing the bishops from the other *civitates* within their provinces.

As well as the bishops recorded in the church council's records, several are mentioned on inscriptions found on archaeological finds. The best example is the text inscribed onto the base of the silver dish known as the Risley Park Lanx. This rectangular plate was found and first published by the noted antiquary William Stukeley. Although the original was then lost, a copy of the lanx, probably made from the recast metal of the original reappeared in 1991. The dish depicted a boar hunt surrounded by a frieze showing other hunting and pastoral scenes. The crucial inscription was scratched onto the back of the dish; it read EXUPEROIS EPISCO[P]US EC(C)LESIAE BOGIENSI DEDIT and finished with a simple *chi-rho* symbol (**8**). Part of the translation is clear, 'Bishop Exuperius gave [this] to . . .,' but a range of alternatives have been suggested to complete the translation: '. . . to the church of [town called] Bogium', '. . . to the church of [a person called] Bogius' or '. . . to the church on Bogius' estate'. Although it was originally thought that the dish was made on the continent it is now clear that it is of

British manufacture, and thus the Bishop Exuperius referred to must have been a British bishop. The precise nature of who or what Bogius was remains unclear. Catherine Potter and Kenneth Painter have suggested that the 'ecclesia' mentioned in the inscription did not refer to a simple low-status church, but to a cathedral.

Another inscription on an object, which appears to record a bishop, was written on a lead salt-pan from Shavington (Cheshire). This object had been cut into eight pieces, but it was clear that it was originally a lead tray used for the drying of the salt from the local Cheshire brine wells (**9**). The remains of the inscription reading VIVENTI [ ]SCOPI were cast in low relief on the inside of the vessel. It is most likely that this second word was EPISCOPI. The text can thus be translated either 'Of Viventius, the bishop' or 'Of Viventius, in the charge of the bishop'. The name Viventius is uncommon, but appears to be associated with Christianity; the female version of the name, Viventia, appears on the Christian Water Newton treasure. A final, less certain, inscription mentioning a bishop comes from the base of a pewter bowl found on the Isle of Ely (Cambs.). This round bowl has an octagonal rim and a pedestal foot. The rim was decorated with a *chi-rho* symbol flanked by an alpha and omega. The inscription was scratched onto the underside of the rim in a very unclear hand. One reading of this text was SUPE(LLE)CTILI EP(ISCOP)I CLERIQUE meaning 'this belongs to/for the furnishings of the bishop and the clergy' (**10**). However, an alternative reading was put forward by the same person as SUPER(A)TI SIC PATIENTIA meaning 'Conquered thus by patience', which makes less sense considering its context. A final reading suggests that the letters merely record a personal name.

Whilst we cannot be sure how many of these subsidiary bishops there were, it is clear that, within a year of the Edict of Milan, Britain had a distinct episcopal hierarchy. It is unlikely that this was a new structure imposed in AD 313, and it is a clear indicator of a Christian church with bishops in many of the major cities. The presence of bishops in each province also shows that the religion was geographically widespread, if not necessarily deep rooted. However, despite his ability to bring in bishops from all areas of the Empire Constantine failed in his attempt to resolve the Donatist dispute, which was still to plague the church in the late fourth century.

An unusual written reference to Christianity comes from a small lead tablet found in the hot spring in Bath (**11**). In the Roman period this was the site of a major temple to the goddess Sulis Minerva. The practice of inscribing vows, wishes and curses on small lead tablets appears to have been not uncommon in Britain at this time. As well as the substantial group from Bath, another large collection was found at temple of Mercury in Uley (Glos.), and they are known from several other temple sites. The texts were usually written in a rough cursive handwriting, rather than the capitals used on formal inscriptions. The tablet in question was written by or on behalf of

E·XVꝑERIV·S·E·ꝑIS CC VꝸECꟿ·ESIꟼ·EꞏBOꞆIEꞏNS IDE DIT··✳

8 *The inscription from the base of the Risley Park Lanx.*
Drawing by Mike Bishop from Mawer, 1995

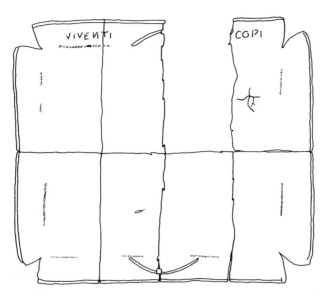

9 *Reassembled fragments of the salt-pan from Shavington Cheshire. It is shown from beneath.* Penny & Shotter, 1996

10 *Inscription scratched on the base of a pewter vessel of the Isle of Ely.* Drawing by Mike Bishop from Mawer, 1995

11 *Lead curse tablet from a hot spring in Bath.* Drawing by Mike Bishop from Mawer, 1995 a certain Annianus, and was an attempt to identify and punish the person who had stolen money from him. The text read in full:

> Whether pagan or Christian, whosoever whether man or woman, whether boy or girl, whether slave or free has stolen from me, Annianus, in the morning six silver pieces from my purse, you, lady Goddess, are to exact [them] from him. If through some deceit he has given me (. . .) and do not give thus to him, but (. . .) his blood who has invoked this on me.

For us the importance is clearly in the first line. Dating to sometime in the fourth century, this is the first surviving case of the word CHRISTIANUS from Britain. Although found in a pagan shrine it is notable that the phrase 'whether pagan or Christian' implies that at the time it was written the author viewed Christianity as having a distinct position as a religion that other religions did not.

Constantine was not content to continue his predecessors' short-lived dreams of a tetrarchy, and he clearly saw Licinius as a continuing political rival. After an initial battle in AD 316 there was an uneasy peace until Constantine defeated his rival in AD 324 at Chrysopolis in Asia Minor. Whilst the Edict of Milan had been issued in the names of both emperors once Constantine assumed total control he had the full power to carry out his Christianising agenda. Until the defeat of his rival, many of his actions had only been effective in the Western Empire. This was one of the failings of both the Council of Rome and the Council of Arles. His intention to become involved in all aspects of the governance of the Church had already been announced by his involvement in these councils.

It was only in AD 325 that he was able to summon a Church council, which really could make a claim to being a universal or 'ecumenical' council. The intention was that its results should be binding upon all members of the Church. This council was not called to deal with the problem of Donatism, but the growing problem of Arianism. Donatism was technically a schism, as it did not involve disagreement over fundamental matters of doctrine. However, its opponents saw Arianism as a full-blown heresy, reflecting deep divisions over the basic matters of faith. The core of the dispute revolved around how the Holy Trinity was perceived. Arius, a priest from Alexandria, argued that God the Son was distinct and secondary to God the Father. His opponents argued that all three aspects of the Trinity were mystically one, the same and equal. The council settled the dispute against Arius, and those who refused to acquiesce in the council's judgements were exiled, an imperial rather than ecclesiastical sanction. However, this was not to be the end of the matter; Arianism came back strongly as Constantine's sons were supporters of Arianism, and Constantine himself was baptised by an Arian bishop shortly before his death. However, due to the great efforts by Athanasius, Bishop of

Alexandria in the Eastern Empire and Hilary of Poitiers in the west it was finally defeated in the Council of Constantinople (AD 381). Athanasius noted the presence of British bishops at Nicaea, and Hilary mentioned the support he had received from them in his struggle against Arianism, showing that British bishops were actively involved in the wider, doctrinal disputes that characterised so much of fourth-century Christianity.

British involvement in wider Church politics continued throughout the fourth century. Athanasius recorded that they attended the Council of Serdica (Bulgaria) in AD 343. They were also at the Council of Ariminium (Italy), where they were recorded accepting state hospitality and use of the state post system to allow them to attend this council. This has sometimes been produced as evidence that the British Church was impoverished, and unable to pay its way. However, as Simon Esmonde Cleary has noted, this was recorded by Sulpicius Severus, a close associate of the ascetic Bishop of Tours Martin. This may well have been an attempt by Sulpicius to emphasise the holy poverty of the British bishops, and a decision to burden the state rather than the Church with expenses of their travel.

Although Christianity made its great breakthrough with the Edict of Milan there were still many bumps on its road to universal acceptance. Although Constantine promoted the religion, there was no significant move to persecute minorities and he was also particularly favourable to Judaism, a sign of his general approval of monotheistic religions. The greatest challenge Christianity had to its burgeoning popularity was the succession of a pagan emperor, Julian (AD 361-3). Julian had been brought up as a Christian, and only returned to paganism after members of the House of Constantine murdered his male relatives. His vision of paganism was more akin to that of Aurelian or pre-conversion Constantine than the traditional more chaotic polytheism of the early Empire. He envisioned a hierarchy of gods with Sol (Sun in Latin)/Helios (Sun in Greek), whom he also equated with Mithras, at its head. Under the influence of the Christian Church Julian appears to have tried to develop a coherent theology. He wrote several anti-Christian polemics, but the extent of his active persecution of Christianity appears to have been limited. He removed tax privileges from the clergy and issued an edict forbidding Christians to teach rhetoric and grammar. He also made an attempt to rebuild the great temple at Jerusalem, possibly in an attempt to refute Jesus' prophecy about its destruction. It will never be known how successful Julian's plan to roll back the Christian Church and replace it with an organised pagan religion would have been. His short reign came to an end in AD 363, when he died whilst campaigning against the Persians. His reformist religious beliefs did not survive him, and his short-lived successor Jovian returned the official support of the Empire to Christianity.

We have little textual evidence for Christianity in Britain for the second half of the fourth century AD, though some events may be inferred. It is clear that

Christians were holding high posts within the government of the diocese. Although we have few details of members of the imperial civil service in Britain from this period, the evidence that does exist points towards the presence of high-status and well-connected Christians. The noted teacher of rhetoric and tutor to the young emperor Gratian, Ausonius (c.AD 310-93/4) corresponded with the Flavius Sanctus, a governor of one of the British provinces. He was not the only important Christian known to have held a post in Britain. In the late fourth or early fifth century a certain Chryanthus was *vicar* of the diocese of Britain. His father had been a bishop of Constantinople, and he himself later became a bishop of the same city.

After Jovian's death Valentinian I became Emperor, initiating a period of dynastic rule, as he was succeeded by his brother and then son. Although a Christian, he was praised by the pagan writer Ammianus Marcellinus for his tolerant attitude towards paganism. This may have been an attempt to ease the transfer of power from Julian's reign. However, under Gratian an increasing amount of anti-pagan legislation began to be passed. Gratian and his successor Theodosius were increasingly influenced in their religious policy by Ambrose, the Bishop of Milan, where the imperial court was now located. At one point he even denied Theodosius Communion after he had ordered a massacre in Thessalonica. It was under his encouragement that Gratian ordered the removal of the altar of victory from the senate house, a truly symbolic incident, reflecting a direct attack on the largely pagan senatorial classes that still dominated Rome. It had previously been removed by Constantius II in AD 353/4, but had probably been replaced by Julian. However, despite the discontent amongst the pagan aristocracy of Rome, Gratian was in fact brought down by a rebellion led by a militantly hard-line Christian. Magnus Maximus was raised to the throne by his armies in Britain in AD 383. He had previous contacts in Britain from when he had campaigned with the elder Count Theodosius against a barbarian invasion in AD 367, and was in Britain again fighting an invasion by Picts and Scots in northern Britain. Maximus led his army to Gaul, where Gratian was caught and executed. A new imperial court was established in Trier, and he took control of the entire prefecture of the Gauls, including Spain and Britain. It was at this point his extreme promotion of religious orthodoxy came to the fore. Priscillanism was a heresy that had taken particular hold in Spain, where the orthodox Church felt extremely threatened by it. Gratian had already commenced action against it before his death, and Maximus continued to oppose it. He called a synod at Bordeaux in AD 384 and the leading figure of the heresy, Bishop Instantius, was deposed. Priscillan, the figurehead of the movement appealed personally to Maximus in Trier. However, despite the intervention of St Martin of Tours, Priscillan was tried, found guilty of magic and put to death with several of his supporters. It was only through a second appeal by Martin that military tribunals – who were on their way to Spain to destroy the heresy – were recalled. Many saw this direct involvement by the emperor in issues of heresy and belief as extremely worrying, and Maximus was condemned by Ambrose, Martin and the Pope Siricius.

Paganism clearly still continued to be extremely widespread and Theodosius was still making laws forbidding pagan sacrifices as late as AD 392. It was this increased pressure against pagans which may have provoked a revolt against Theodosius in AD 391. This was defeated at the battle of the River Frigidus, which was seen by many Christians as a divine judgement on the pagan cause.

After the death of Theodosius in AD 395 the Roman Empire was shared between his two sons Arcadius, who ruled the East and Honorius who controlled the West. In the late fourth and early fifth centuries Britain became increasingly vulnerable to raiding from the Picts in Scotland and from the Scots, based in Ireland, raiding along the west coast. Although these raids were increasing in strength, Britain was slowly being denuded of its military garrisons, as troops were removed to fight against the tribes attacking the Empire, elsewhere in Europe and in the East. Although Honorius was nominally in charge in the west, the real power was held by his *magister militum* (master of soldiers) Flavius Stilicho, a Vandal married to Theodosius' niece and adoptive daughter. His daughter was also married to Honorius. His control of the armies and his dynastic connections gave him tremendous power. His military successes included defeats of the Saxons, Scots and Picts in AD 398 and AD 400. However, before, during and after these victories, troops were being removed from Britain to face threats from the Visigoths amongst others. With Stilicho increasingly focusing his field of operations in Italy, a series of military revolts occurred in Britain. The army first raised and then murdered a soldier named Marcus. He was followed by a native Romano-Briton named Gratian; he too was soon murdered. However, with the real or perceived threat of a further barbarian invasion increasing, the next leader to be elevated by the British armies, Constantine III, lasted a little longer. With his two sons, Julian and Constans, he quickly imposed his authority on Gaul. He based himself in Arles and controlled the entire Gallic prefecture having seen off moves against him by Honorius' armies. However, at around the same time he was recognised by Honorius, he was faced by a rebellion from his British *magister militum* Gerontius, who provoked barbarian attacks on Gaul leading to wider attacks on Gaul and Britain. In the face of these attacks the chronicler Zosimus records that the invasions 'brought the people of Britain (. . .) to the point where they revolted from Roman rule and lived by themselves, no longer obeying Roman laws. The Britons took up arms and fighting for themselves, freed the cities from the barbarian pressure.' This more than anything marks the end of Roman political control of Britain.

There is good reason to believe that many of the main players in these final years of Roman Britain were Christian. Although it is dangerous to argue from negative evidence, it is noticeable that none were noted as pagan in any of the contemporary chronicles. In an era when the choice of personal names was of great ideological importance, and new names could often be assumed, both Gratian and Constantine, both indicated an identification with earlier Christian emperors. There is other evidence to suggest that Constantine III was a Christian; following his defeat by Honorius' general, Constantius had himself ordained before surrendering. Whilst this was undoubtedly an attempt to get the privileges of protection held by the clergy, he would have needed to be already baptised to be able to be ordained. Orosius also records that his son Constans was a monk. If Gratian was a Christian this has important implications for the state of Christianity in Britain, as he was a civilian and presumably drawn from the local ruling class.

Gratian is not the only member of the late Romano-British municipal ruling class to have probably been Christian. The only written testimony of a Romano-British Christian, the *Confessions of St Patrick*, attests to at least three generations of Christians in his family. Although only known from later versions, Patrick's spiritual biography records that his father was a *decurio* (a member of the governing council of a town) of Bannaven Taburniae, the nearest town to the small estate (*villula*) on which his family lived. However, as well as having this secular position, his father, Calpurnius, was also a deacon, whilst his grandfather had been a priest. The precise location of Patrick's home is debatable, though Charles Thomas has suggested that Bannaven Taburniae can be identified as the civilian settlement (*vicus*) of the Roman fort of Birdoswald (*Banna*) on Hadrian's Wall. As well as these Christian members of the decurion class, some larger absentee landowners were also followers of the religion. One owner of estates in Britain and elsewhere was the ascetic noblewoman Melania the Younger, a member of a senatorial family who also owned estates in Campania, Apulia, Sicily, Africa, Numidia and Mauretania. The extent to which she would have exerted control over religious practice on her estates is uncertain, though it is known that at least one of her estates in Africa had its own bishop.

Another middle or upper ranking Christian Briton was the priest Pelagius, originator of the Pelagian heresy, which was to concern the greatest minds of the late fourth- and early fifth-century church. This heresy denied the notion of 'original sin', and critiqued the concept of 'grace'. Rather than seeing salvation as being solely attainable through God he was influenced by pagan philosophy, especially Stoicism, in believing that moral strength was enough to achieve paradise. He believed that Jesus had saved man by providing a good example and giving instruction that counterbalanced the bad example given by Adam. His greatest opponent was St Augustine, whose own theology was developing an emphasis on Divine Will and the grace of God.

The precise date of Pelagius' birth is uncertain, but he was in Rome studying law in the 380s, where, in around 386 he gave up the law and became a priest. He would presumably thus have been born in the second half of the fourth century, probably in the 360s. Although he is not thought to have returned to Britain, it is his early years that are most informative. The fact that he had the education and financial backing to attempt to pursue a legal career implies that he must have come from a prosperous background in Britain. There is nothing in the records of his move from the law courts to the Church that suggests that this move included conversion, and he was presumably already Christian when he arrived in Rome.

References to Christianity in Britain continue to be found in the very late fourth and early fifth century. At some point in the 390s, possibly 396, Victricius, the archbishop of *Rotamagus* (Rouen) travelled to Britain. In his own words: 'if I have gone to Britain, if I have stayed there, it is to carry out your own orders. The bishops, my brothers in the priesthood, called on me to make peace there. Could I, your soldier, have refused them?' (*De Laude Sanctorum* i.) The exact cause of the dissension amongst the British Church is unclear. It has been frequently suggested that it may have been an attempt to combat the Pelagian heresy, but there is no direct evidence for this. Whatever the cause of his journey, it must have been of great import; as a metropolitan bishop Victricius was an extremely important figure in the Christian hierarchy in Gaul. His role as a peacemaker and settler of ecclesiastical disputes continued and in AD 403 received an important letter known as *Liber Regularum* from Pope Innocent I, which dealt with a range of questions about ecclesiastical practice and discipline.

If the disputes dealt with by Victricius were not Pelagian in origin, those dealt with by Germanus, another Gaulish bishop certainly were. The chronicler Prosper described the reason for his first trip to Britain in AD 429: 'The Pelagian Agricola, son of the Pelagian Bishop Severianus, corrupts the churches of Britain by the propagation of his doctrines. But at the instigation of the deacon Palladius, Pope Celestine sends Germanus, Bishop of Auxerre, in his stead, who overthrows the heretics and guides the Britons to the Catholic faith.' Germanus, Bishop of Auxerre, was accompanied by another Bishop, Lupus of Troyes. As well as Prosper's note of their visit, the story is also told in the *Passio Albani* (see above), and *Vita Germani*, a chronicle of Germanus' life written by Constantius of Lyons, probably around AD 480. Like other saints lives of this time it includes many motifs and stories derived from biblical and other early Christian sources. Even one or two of the basic details differ from what we are told elsewhere; for example, according to the *Vita*, it is the British themselves who ask for help in combating Pelagianism. However, the basic outline of their trip is clear. After crossing the Channel and travelling through the countryside, a large crowd, including supporters of the Pelagian heresy, meets them. These Pelagians are recorded as being richly dressed, though it is not clear whether this was because they were of high-status, or more likely, an attempt by Constantius to represent them as vain and overbearing. Also amongst the crowd was a man with the rank of Tribune. Germanus cured his daughter of blindness. This may well have been an allegorical representation of his freeing of Britain of heresy, in which case the tribune may have been a purely symbolic figure. Following a debate, the Pelagians are defeated. A later reference in another work by Prosper suggests that Pope Celestine may have authorised Germanus to exile them. Following this defeat the Germanus and Lupus both made a journey to the tomb of Alban. After a number of inevitable miracles on their return home they are called to help the British in a conflict against the Saxons and the Picts. After baptising the British troops Germanus leads them to a miraculous victory achieved through crying 'Alleluiah' three times. This again is strongly resonant of biblical stories, particular Joshua's battle at Jericho (*Joshua* 6, 1-20). The *Vita* mentions a second visit not recorded elsewhere. Its precise dates are not clear, AD 435, 437 and 445-8 have all been suggested, though it is quite possible that this second visit did not occur at all and was merely a result of confusion on the part of Constantius. Certainly the events recorded are pretty desultory. Accompanied this time by Severus, Germanus returns to Britain on hearing of the return of Pelagianism. On arrival it is soon apparent that this revival of the heresy is of a small scale, but he still defeats it, and after further miracles returns to Gaul with the blessings of the British bishops.

The British Church is also mentioned in a work known as 'On the Seven Offices of the Church', which was probably written in the mid-fifth century, and deals with various issues related to the role of priests. In particular, it addresses whether priests should be allowed to preach, which in Gaul was the sole remit of bishops. In a list of places where priests were allowed to preach Britain was mentioned. This is important as it implies both knowledge of the pastoral duties of British priests and also a divergence in practice between Britain and Gaul.

British Christianity continues to make appearances in Gaulish texts through the fifth century, though it is increasingly difficult to distinguish references to events in Britain from those in Brittany. For example, in AD 461 an 'episcopus Brittanorum' named Mansuetus is recorded as attending a church council in Tours. It is not certain whether he was indeed a British bishop who was fortuitously in town, perhaps on pilgrimage to the shrine of St Martin, or if instead he ministered to a British community settled in Gaul. The consensus now appears to be the latter. Léon Fleuriot identified him with a Chariato (a name which like Mansuetus means 'charitable') who attended a council at Angers in AD 453. Another, more certainly British Christian, is Bishop Fastidius, who is mentioned in the continuation of St Jerome's *De Viris Illustribus* (On Illustrious Men), which was made by Gennadius of Marseille at the end of the fifth century. His brief entry reads: 'Fastidius, bishop in Britain, wrote to one Fatalis, a book On the Christian life, and another On preserving the estate of virginity, a work full of sound doctrine, and doing honour to God' (DVI 67).

Chronologically Gennadius places Fastidius between the reigns of Pope Celestine I (d. 432) and Cyril (d. 444). Fastidius was associated at times with Pelagianism, and the Fatalis to which he wrote may have been the same man addressed in a letter by Pelagius. If so this suggests that Germanus' fight against Pelagianism in AD 429 may not have been as successful as he believed.

At least two more British Christians are recorded in the correspondence of Sidonius Apollinaris (c.AD 430-80), originally a wealthy landowner in Aquitaine who became Bishop of Clermont-Ferrand. He was a great letter writer and moved in a circle of Christian writers, holy men and intellectuals in Western Gaul. He appears to have also been in contact with British Christians. In his letters he mentions Faustus, who from AD 462 was Bishop of Riez. Although his active life was spent in Gaul (he was a monk at Lérins before becoming bishop) both Sidonius and Avitus, Bishop of Vienne, record that he was of British origin. It was clear that he continued to have close contacts with the British Church. Sidonius writes to Faustus of a visit by a certain Riocatus, a 'priest and monk' (*antistes et monachus*) who was returning a book to Britain on behalf of Faustus, and mentions that he too was British. Intriguingly, both Riocatus and Faustus were known in the later early medieval tradition in Britain. Faustus was recorded in the ninth-century *Historia Brittonum* as the fourth son of Vortigern (*HB* 48), and Riocatus as his grandson (*HB* 49), though the truth behind these records is dubious.

The Bible

The pre-eminent Christian book is, of course, the Bible. However, at this time the Bible did not exist in the form we know it today. The term used by St Jerome, the most important translator of the Bible, was *Bibliotheca Divina* (the Divine Library). As this suggests, the Bible at this time was a disparate collection of religious works, rather than one solid volume. It is important to distinguish between the writing of a work and its later acceptance as part of the 'canon' (from the Greek for 'a rule'). The contents of the Old Testament used by Christians was taken from the Greek translation of the Hebrew canon, known as the Septuagint, which had probably been completed in the third century BC. It included several writings not founding the traditional Hebrew canon. These were the 'apocrypha', which were accepted as part of the Bible by most early Christian Churches, but not by the Jews. It had become accepted as the basis for the Old Testament as it was the version used by the heavily Greek-influenced Jewish communities amongst which early Christianity developed.

Unlike the Old Testament, the New Testament was being written as the Church was developing. It did not appear as a pre-packaged collection. The earliest writings, such as the first gospels, were read by Christians as recording the foundation of their Church, but there was no sense that they were to provide a distinct New Testament, which would complement the Septuagint. At this early period much Christian teaching would rely as much on eyewitness testimony as the written word. However, from the late first to second century certain writings were commonly being collected together for use in the small communities of the Christian diaspora. That said, the precise contents of these collections still varied. As well as the four gospels of Matthew, Mark, Luke and John, other gospels were also circulated, such as the Gospel of Truth. Importantly, these early writings, particularly the Gospels and the letters of St Paul, were beginning to be included into elements of religious worship, not unlike the books of the Septuagint.

The idea of a formal collection of Christian books only came in the later second century – the earliest version including only the gospel of Luke and ten letters of Paul, although the rest of the gospels and all of Paul's letters were soon added. However, there was still a good deal of uncertainty as to the rest of the contents of the New Testament. New gospels continued to appear and there were still many peripheral works, which had some claim to be included. It was only in 367 that Athanasius, the archbishop of Alexandria, outlined a list of books that included all those now found in the New Testament. Even this took a while to be universally accepted. It may have been accepted in the Western Church at the Synod of Rome in 382, but was only certainly confirmed in 405.

Because of the slow development of the Bible there was no one authoritative translation of it. Whilst the Latin versions of the Old Testament were uniformly based on the Septuagint, the books of the New Testament were known in many variant forms. Until the late fourth century this group of disparate translations was known together as the *Vetus Latina* (Old Latin). Even within the *Vetus Latina* there were different versions circulating, including a Gallic one and a North African one. However, from the 380s over the course of nearly twenty years St Jerome retranslated all these works, returning to the original Hebrew for the Old Testament. This new work was known as the *versio vulgata* (common translation), or as it is usually called today, the Vulgate. It took some time for this Vulgate to replace the *Vetus Latina*. In the few examples of biblical knowledge we have from Britain it is the *Vetus* that is represented. St Patrick certainly mainly used the *Vetus*, as did Gildas writing around 100 years later. However, there are hints from both writers that they were aware of the Vulgate translation, even if they did not use it extensively.

Even if by the end of the fourth century the contents of the Bible had become circumscribed, and the Church was fixing on one translation, there were still practical differences between the book then, and as we know it now. Today, when we look at a Bible we see all the elements bound together in a single volume. In the fourth century this would not have been the case. The time and cost of a complete hand-written version of the Bible would have been far outside the resources of most churches, especially ones of limited funds. Instead, most churches are likely to have only a few elements of the complete work, such as the Gospels and the Psalter, which contained the Psalms and much of the liturgy, the instructions for worship.

Conclusions

The historical evidence for Christianity in Roman Britain is small compared to the amount of textual evidence for early Christianity in Gaul or North Africa. It is almost all derived from sources written outside Britain, and only deals with topics of interest to foreign writers. It shows that the British Church was closely integrated with the wider family of Roman Churches. British bishops can be seen participating in the major Church council of the period, and being actively involved in dealing with major issues, such as heresy. As well as official involvement in the administration of the faith, British bishops are also shown to have a range of other links, particularly with Gaul. The visit of Victricius and Germanus shows the Gaulish Church was closely interested in the activities of its insular cousins. The fifth-century references to books being returned to Britain from Gaul also gives us a tantalising insight into some of the less official contacts between the two churches, showing that links were maintained as much through friendship and scholarly exchange as through official or administrative channels.

However, the historical evidence only gives us occasional insights into the day-to-day life of Romano-British Christians. Frustratingly, the one authentic testimony of a fourth-century British Christian, St Patrick's Confessions, primarily deal with events outside the diocese. Invaluable as the historical information is, it is to the archaeological evidence we must turn if we want to get a proper understanding of Christianity in Roman Britain.

3

THE CHURCH

The growing number of Christians in Roman Britain faced one important challenge, finding somewhere to worship. Whether searching for a secure and discreet meeting place during the persecutions or a spacious home for a burgeoning congregation in the mid-fourth century there has always been a need for a physical space in which the Christian communities could practice their beliefs. Unlike the medieval world, Roman Britain was not provided with a dense network of parish churches, instead there appears to have been an uneven and inconsistent coverage of the country with a range of different types of church structure.

The modern use of the word 'church' for both the physical building and the wider community of worshipper was not necessarily reflected in the Latin of Roman Britain. The term *ecclesia*, coming from the Greek for a 'select assembly' was certainly used to describe church buildings on mainland Europe, but we have little evidence for its use in fourth-century Britain. However, this may have been due to the paucity of contemporary texts of any kind from Britain in this period. The *Confessio* of St Patrick, the only first-person document written by a Late Roman Christian, certainly does not use the term. One term which may have been used to describe Christian places of worship is found on an inscription from the Christian Water Newton hoard: SANCTUM ALTARE TUUM DOMINE SUBNIXUS HONORO meaning literally 'I humbly honour your holy altar, O Lord'. It is likely that the term *altare*, not a word commonly used to describe pagan altars, was used in a metaphorical sense to describe the church building as a whole. The small silver bowl on which these words were carved was presumably given as an offering to adorn the church to which it referred.

The liturgy of the Eucharist

To better understand the nature of churches in Roman Britain it is important to comprehend in more detail the role of the church in the Christian community. It would have had overlapping roles, as meeting place, place of group worship and solitary prayer. However, the main role of the church was for the celebration of the sacrament of the Eucharist, the central rite of the Christian Church. It is in this ceremony, a ritualised re-enactment of the Last Supper, that the Christian congregations would come together with a common purpose to affirm their core beliefs and remember the sequence of events leading up to Jesus' crucifixion and resurrection. The Last Supper was of course itself a ritualised event, as it was a celebration of the pre-existing Jewish *pesach* (Passover) ceremony.

This celebration of the Eucharist changed significantly over the first four hundred years of Christianity. The earliest evidence we have for the celebration of the events comes from New Testament, where St Paul refers to the importance of the semi-formalised partaking of bread and wine (1 Corinthians 11: 20-34). This simple supper became increasingly formalised in the following years; the words and rites used began to be written down and there were attempts at imposing uniformity. In the earliest years, the format of the celebration of the Eucharist was probably determined by the local bishop, although the Metropolitan bishop of the diocese may have exerted some wider influence over the rites. Simple texts and prayers to be used in the Eucharist were being written down from the end of the first century AD, for example in the Greek text the *Didache* (known in the Latin West as *De doctrinâ Apostolorum* – the Doctrines of the Apostles) and in the writings of the apologist Justin Martyr (d. *c*.AD 164) who recorded the rites he saw in Rome in the mid-second century AD. In the fourth century AD there was an increased move towards centralisation of these rites, and there was a crystallisation of the anarchic range of rituals to four main broad streams; the liturgies of Antioch, Alexandria, Rome and Gaul. The Church in Britain almost certainly followed this latter, Gallican rite. It was ultimately the conflict between this rite and the Roman rite brought by St Augustine that led to the Synod of Whitby in AD 664.

Bringing together these various sources, and allowing for variation over time and space, it is possible to outline the basic pattern of the early Christian church service, which contained the ceremony of the Eucharist:

1. Readings from the Old and New Testaments
2. Sermon by the bishop
3. Prayers for all the people
4. Kiss of peace
5. Offering of bread and wine and water brought up by the deacons
6. Thanksgiving prayer by the bishop
7. Consecration by the words of institution
8. Intercession for the people
9. The people end this prayer with *Amen*
10. The taking of bread and wine

This service was divided into two distinct sections. The first part, the readings and the sermon was known as the *Mass of the Catechumens*, which was open to all members of the church, whether full members or not. However, the following section, *Mass of the Faithful,* was open only to those who had been baptised. Those not allowed to attend were forced to withdraw to a separate area for further instruction.

From these simple schemes we can better understand the demands placed upon early church buildings. Certain physical attributes would be needed: a place from where the readings could be made, an altar at which the Eucharist could be celebrated and to which the bread, wine and water could be brought, as well as space for the offertory procession. In addition, a separate space for the celebrants of the mass and enough room for the whole celebrating congregation. We know from parallels elsewhere that the bishop would have had a special chair, known as a *cathedra*. There may also have been a subsidiary space to which the unbaptised could withdraw (the *vestibulum*).

Earliest church buildings

When the Church was first established, just as the earliest rites were not fully formalised, neither was the design for the meeting places. It is thought that most meetings took place in the houses of worshippers. The sporadic phases of persecution of Christian acted as a break on moves towards official, purpose built churches. These early meeting places would have been indistinguishable from normal residential houses, and it is not surprising that we cannot recognise any of these early proto-churches in Britain.

From the mid-second century AD the nascent Christian Church was growing in strength. Although still not strong in Britain, elsewhere in the Empire congregations were expanding. By AD 250, the number of Christians in Rome probably numbered between 30,000 and 50,000, and in Africa and Asia Minor there may have even been a slight majority of Christian worshippers. As well as increasing in numbers, the profile of the community was changing, including more wealthy and high status individuals. These factors led to an increased level of organisation amongst the congregations and a growth of a professional clergy. In the middle of the third century, despite occasional continued periods of persecution, the Church existed in the open. This provided the opportunity for the growth of more permanent meeting places. The physical structures of the church houses (*domus ecclesiae*) were altered to provide permanent rooms given over to Christian worship. Whilst several of these house churches have been excavated both in Rome and elsewhere in the Empire, none have been recognised in Britain. Again, this is perhaps not surprising. Despite their alterations, these buildings continued to be at heart domestic buildings. The best-preserved house church, excavated in

Dura Europos in Syria, included a series of overtly Christian wall paintings. However, if it was known from only its plan, as most Romano-British houses are, there would have been nothing to indicate that it was a place of Christian worship. On the Continent it has also been possible to recognise house-churches, which have become incorporated into later Christian churches; again no such survivals have been found in Britain.

When the Edict of Milan in AD 313 regularised the position of Christianity in the Roman Empire, the Church had its first real opportunity, both in terms of legal position and financial backing to create purpose-built churches. The Church could have turned to pre-existing traditions of religious building when it was searching for the appropriate architectural forms for Christian churches. The Roman Empire was full of pagan temples, shrines and meeting places. The typical classical form of temple with a central portico was rare in Britain, with a few notable exceptions, such as the Temple of Claudius in Colchester. More common was the native Romano-Celtic form of temple. These usually took the form of simple squares or more rarely circular or octagonal buildings surrounded by a concentric ambulatory, around which the worshippers may have processed. This structure – and sometime other building – was then surrounded by a large outer enclosure known as a *temenos*. Although, as we shall see later, some churches were superficially similar in form to these Romano-Celtic temples, on the whole Christians rejected architectural forms perceived as pagan. There appears to have been a need to mark a break with the pagan past, and create an entirely new architectural vocabulary for religious architecture. Instead, they turned to the pre-existing Roman tradition of civic, administrative architecture.

The new relationship between the Church and the state led to the role of the bishops, the leaders of the church, being restated in a new way. The bishop was no longer a leader of an illegal and potentially subversive sect, but God's representative on earth. In the same way that Roman magistrates were the public face of the emperor in the towns and provinces of the Empire, the bishop was the public face of God, the emperor of Heaven, in this world. The parallel between bishops and magistrates was increasingly explicitly drawn. Unsurprisingly, this tendency influenced the design and layout of churches. In particular, the Church adopted a widespread building plan, the basilica.

The basilical structure is simple in form. It consists of a rectangular hall with an apse or rectangular area at the end, which was the focus of the structure. Many were divided lengthways into a central nave and subsidiary aisles by columns. The nave was often lit by a series of windows supported by these columns, which thus let light into the main body of the church, but not the aisles. There may also have been windows in the main walls of the church. The timber roof may have been open or concealed above a flat ceiling. The basilica was a venerable building design, with its roots reaching back into the first century AD and even earlier. Its initial function was usually as a meeting hall, and was most widely found as part of the complex of buildings associated with the forum, the central market place, of most Roman towns. As well as acting as a central meeting place it also housed the magistrates who oversaw the administration of the town. They would have sat on a raised platform at the apse end of the building.

By taking over the form of the basilica for early churches, Christians were absorbing an architectural form that would have had strong redolences for most Romans. It was a type of building already used for expressing social, political and judicial power; adding a spiritual dimension is the obvious next step. Indeed, the Christians were not the first religious group to utilise the basilical form. In the third century other groups of worshippers, such as the followers of Mithras began using basilicas for their temples. Several good examples of Mithraic temples in this form are known in Britain from along the northern frontier of Hadrian's Wall, such as that at Carrawburgh, a small rectangular building (*c.*7.9m by 5.5m) with side aisles (**12**). Another well-understood Mithraeum has been found at Wallbrook, London, where a rectangular building (18.3m by 7.6m) with an apsidal west end stood. It too had side aisles. However, it is unlikely that Mithraic basilicas could be confused with Christian churches; Mithraic temples tend to have stone

12 *Temple of Mithras at Carrawburgh, Northumberland, showing basilica form*

benches along the sides of the central room, and there is usually evidence not just for a central altar, but also side altars.

Like Christianity and other popular cults of the later Roman Empire, Mithraism had its origin in the Near East. Popular amongst the military, it was extremely hierarchical in nature, with worshippers progressing through a series of ranks as they achieved fuller knowledge of the mysteries of the religion. This basilical form lends itself well to the expression of hierarchies and ranking through the use of space. We have already seen how the presence of a dais and the apse would have served as a focal point for the celebration of the rituals carried out within the building. The distance from this central nexus of the building would have provided a means of expressing rank and status; those nearer the front being the more favoured. The provision of a *narthex* and side aisles, through which visual access to the main body of the building could be enabled and prevented through the use of curtains or doors would have provided another way in which space could be controlled within the church. Textual evidence tells us that in certain parts of the mass, those who had not been baptised would withdraw for instruction, whilst the sacrament of the Eucharist was carried out. The more important and honoured members of the congregation might be expected to have stood near the front of the church, whilst those with less status may have been relegated to the back of the building. Another social division, which may have been reflected in the use of space within the church building, is that of gender. Evidence from elsewhere in the Empire suggests that men and women were often seated in separate areas of the church. Sometimes they sat on different sides of the nave, in other cases men seated at the front, whilst women sat at the back.

Urban churches

Unlike many parts of the Roman Empire, Britain never developed a truly successful urban infrastructure. Although some of the tribal capitals in the south-east of England might be generously called proto-urban, Britain had no urban tradition on the eve of the Roman Conquest. Roman rule led to the plantation and nurturing of a series of towns, which became central nodes in the governance of the province. They acted as hooks over which the network of political, judicial and fiscal administration was hung. As these towns developed they were supplied with the repertoire of buildings that was expected from a Roman town. This included a forum and its associated basilica, baths, temples and perhaps an amphitheatre. Not surprisingly with the increasing growth of Christianity in the fourth century, churches soon appeared in these towns. However, the towns of Roman Britain in the fourth century were not the same as the successful and burgeoning towns of the second century. Although activity still continued in the towns there had been a notable decline in the quantity of new public buildings and the maintenance of existing structures. The practice of subsidising the construction of important civic structures was widespread across much of the Roman Empire, but it appears to have never become truly popular in Britain. After an initial first flush of enthusiasm for urban life in Britain, much of it supported by the Roman state, there was no continued native support for major public building programs. Although there was continued construction in third- and fourth-century Romano-British towns, this tended to be small-scale private, domestic or industrial building. Many of the urban, public complexes, such as forums, basilicas and temples seem to have undergone a major period of change, with their former civic use being replaced by less high-status activity. For example, the basilica at Silchester was given over to metalworking by the end of the third century. It is in this context of declining urban public building that the first churches were built. Considering the general lack of new public buildings within city walls it is not surprising that in Britain there are few probable examples of urban churches.

Perhaps the most certain example of a church is the basilica from the town of *Calleva* (Silchester, Hants.), though even this example has had its identity disputed (**13**). This small building at Silchester lay to the south-east corner of the same insula as the forum and basilica stood. The structure was first excavated by George Fox and W.H. St John Hope in 1892 and was subsequently reinvestigated in 1961. This relatively small building (*c.*13m long and *c.*9m wide) was aligned west-east, about 10m north of the street. The central section was a 4m wide nave with an apsidal end. It was paved with simple red cubes. At the west end, just east of the apse was a contrasting mosaic panel, with a black and white chequered pattern surrounded by a geometric border. To the north and south of the nave were two aisles. The relationship between the nave and these aisles is not certain, though it is likely that the foundations supported a series of equally spaced column bases. The western ends of the aisles may have been separate chambers or transepts, as there are traces of a possible timber doorframe in the northern aisle. This doorframe appears to have been a secondary feature, and originally the aisle may have been open along its full length. A doorway accessing the western end of the nave from this room is also likely. This corner of the building was later rebuilt due to subsidence, and the wooden frame appeared to have been replaced by a masonry screen with a doorway. At the east end of the church running the full width of the structure was a smaller chamber or *narthex*. This had direct access to the nave and possibly the aisles. Like the nave it was paved with a red, tessellated floor. The building was probably entered through this *narthex*, though no threshold is visible close to the north wall of this chamber a hole was cut through the floor. It may have been the footings for a table or plinth.

There is very little dating evidence for this building. It seems to have post-dated a wooden building just to the north, which probably stood until the late

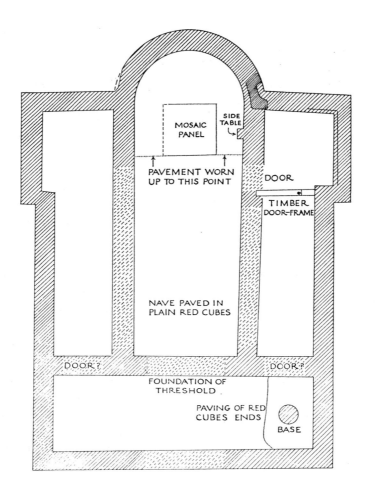

MOSAIC PANEL

SIDE TABLE

PAVEMENT WORN UP TO THIS POINT

DOOR

TIMBER DOOR-FRAME

NAVE PAVED IN PLAIN RED CUBES

DOOR ?

DOOR ?

FOUNDATION OF THRESHOLD

PAVING OF RED CUBES ENDS

BASE

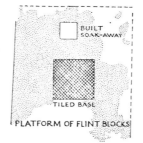

BUILT SOAK-AWAY

TILED BASE

PLATFORM OF FLINT BLOCKS

10m

13 *The Roman church and font base at Silchester*

third century. The mosaic, although simple, has its nearest parallels with an early fourth-century example from Verulamium (St Albans). The structure is likely to have been built sometime between the late third century and the early fourth century. It is possible that the construction of the building could be squeezed into a date bracket after this date, but perhaps not likely. There is some evidence of later, so-called 'squatter occupation' in the church. Again the precise date of this activity is not easy to date, although a small group of coins and fragments of pottery suggests that it did not begin until at least the third quarter of the fourth century.

The precise identification of this building as a church is not certain. There is a lack of any clearly Christian objects. However, there are some architectural clues. The presence of a western apse, rather than an eastern focus for the building, is unusual, but is paralleled in the small early fourth-century church of St Severin from Cologne. One of the more convincing features is the presence of the two transeptal spaces at the west end of the aisles. Sheppard Frere, who published the 1961 excavations, noted that these are hard to find parallels for in secular basilica structures. The function of these areas is unclear; if the building is a church it is possible that the more clearly defined northern room may have been a sacristy. It has also been suggested that it could have a chamber for a relic of martyr. The location of the building within the city walls indicates that the remains of any early martyr would have to have been relocated from an external cemetery location. This practice only began elsewhere in the Empire in the second half of the fourth century, so it would not have been the purpose behind the construction of the church. This, however, may explain the secondary nature of the door screen at the end of the north aisle. If the building is not a church what are the alternatives? One is that the building was a *schola*, the meeting hall for a *collegium*, a quasi-religious guild. Again, however, there is no clear evidence for such an identification. Another alternative is that as the building was constructed at the same time that the main basilica was going out of use it may have taken over some of its functions. A smaller meeting room may have been more appropriate to the decreased powers of a weakened late Roman town council. A final challenge to a Christian identity of the building is the dating evidence. The evidence perhaps points to a late third or early fourth-century construction date, which seems too early for a congregational church.

As with so much of the evidence for early Christian churches the identification of this site is ultimately subjective. The situation is complicated by the possibility that the building may have gone through several phases of use; the addition of the divide in the north aisle being a case in point. It is possible that this may represent a change in function. For the author, the presence of the apsidal end and the unusual transepts suggest a church is the least unlikely explanation for this building. The dating of the building is admittedly a little uncomfortable, but allowing for the extent of residuality from the earlier building on the site and the unsophisticated nineteenth-century excavation of the site which may have truncated much of the overlying dark squatter layer means that the precise period of use for the structure is always going to be uncertain.

The church at Lincoln is one of the best candidates for a late Roman church. It was found during excavations on the site of the medieval parish church of St Paul-in-the-Bail, which was demolished in 1971 (**14**). It was clear before work had begun on the excavations that it was the site first of the headquarters of the first-century Roman legion stationed in the city and later of the town's forum. However, the most unexpected discovery was a series of very early church structures. These stood in the middle of the forum, not over the buildings on the eastern edge. Only the eastern end of the earliest structure was excavated. This measured at least 6m in length and 6m wide. It was divided into two by a north-south trench containing the remains of post-holes. This appeared to mark out a possible rectangular eastern apse. Overlying this was a

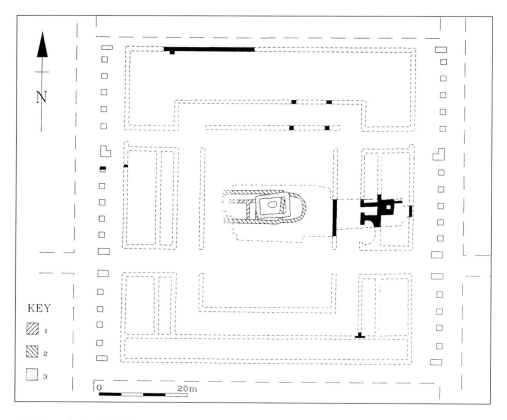

14 *The early church buildings at the site of St Paul-in-the-Bail, Lincoln. The church stands in the central courtyard of the Roman forum.* Jones, 1994

larger structure defined by large foundation trenches, which probably supported a mainly timber structure. The main part of this building was at least 15m long and 8m wide. A large apse was attached on the eastern end. This was slightly narrower than the nave. As with the earlier structure, a north-south trench with post-holes divided the two areas, probably forming a chancel screen of some form. There was no sign of any internal aisles within the main building. It is possible that its western end was attached to the western portico of the forum, which may have formed a simple *narthex*.

The dating of these buildings is difficult. The earliest structure is almost certainly late Roman. A coin found on the floor of the second church belonged to the Emperor Arcadius (AD 388-92) suggesting that it was built in or after *c*.AD 390. The second church was surrounded by, and cut by, a number of burials. These have been radiocarbon dated in an attempt to ascertain a more definite date for the building. Although radiocarbon dating can be quite inaccurate for remains of the late Roman and early medieval period enough measurements were taken to suggest some broad date ranges. These burials are dated to the seventh-eighth century AD, suggesting it had been demolished by this date. Other, earlier burials were found; these had broad fourth- to eighth-century dates, suggesting that the church was in use during this period. A rough sequence of events for the site might be as follows. First, sometime in the second half of the fourth century the earliest structure was built, then in the last decade of the century, the larger, apsidal-ended church was built. Around the same period burials began to appear. Two of the earliest burials were fragmentary, and possibly cut by the chancel wall. Another lay inside the building to the west of this dividing wall. This had an earlier radiocarbon date placing the burial sometime in the mid-Roman period. It is possible that this date was inaccurate; however, if it was precise it is possible that the human remains may have been kept and reburied as holy relics. If true, this confirms a late fourth-century or later date for the church, as the translation of relics in this manner did not begin until this period.

This is not the only potential Christian church in Lincoln. A large basilica was excavated in Flaxengate in the lower town. The site was excavated under difficult circumstances, with much flooding. However, it was possible to get a good picture of the plan of the building. Archaeologists uncovered the north-east corner of a large fourth-century building (**15**). It appeared to be rectangular, and had an apse at the east end. A large masonry standing was found at the junction of the apse and the main east wall. This may have formed the base for a column framing the apse. Based on the excavated area, the structure was probably around 15m wide. To the north of the building was a possible portico running the length of the building floored with rough cobbles. The internal space of the building was floored with tesserae placed in a concrete-like matrix. The building was probably architecturally elaborate, as fragments of decorative marble and wall plaster were found. Once more, there is no direct evidence

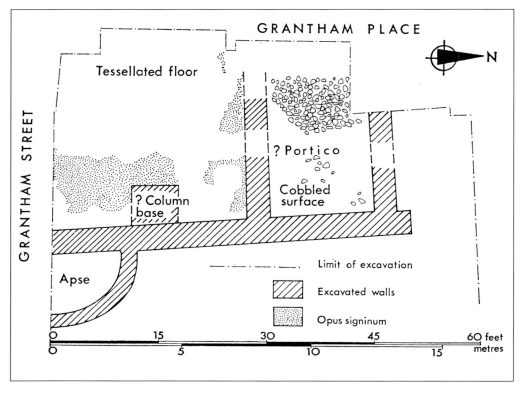

15 *The eastern end of a basilica from Flaxengate, Lincoln.* Colyer & Jones, 1979

that this large basilica was a church. However, its size, and its fourth-century date, must make it a candidate for being a religious building.

Another basilica which has been put forward as a church has been found at *Verulamium* (St Albans). The archaeologists Mortimer and Tessa Wheeler found a small basilical building in the southern area of the town (**16**). It was aligned roughly north-east to south-west, with small rectangular additions at each end. However, this plan with rectangular projections at both ends does not have any clear parallels with church structures from Britain or the Continent. The south-western projection is notably more substantial than any other part of the building, and it is possible that it supported a tower. Although towers may have been an integral part of the medieval church, they were not introduced until the late Anglo-Saxon period. The likelihood that this structure was a church is small.

Although it was the capital of the late Roman diocese of Britannia the structural evidence for Christianity from London is minimal. Until recently there was no evidence at all for any Roman churches within the city walls. However, in excavations carried out in 1992 and 1993 at Colchester House to the north-west of Tower Hill, in the south-east corner of the Roman city, the remains of a large aisled building constructed in the mid-fourth century AD was found. However, the remains of this structure were fragmentary in the extreme, consisting of occasional fragments of walls and foundation pads for possible columns (**17**). The remains of most of the walls had been robbed out leaving only traces of the once substantial foundations. From these slight traces a possible plan of part of the structure has been reconstructed. It was aligned west-east and parts of a large northern wall, with foundations over 2m wide running were seen. A slightly narrower wall running southwards at right angles from this first wall was also identified. To the south of this second wall and on the same alignment was a large post-pad foundation. To the east of this wall were the remains of a further group of six post-pads arranged in two rows. Traces of two pads on a similar alignment were also found to the west of the north-south wall. The excavators have reconstructed these remains to form the north-east corner of large basilical building. The north-south wall may have separated a smaller western area from the main body of the structure, with the southern post-pad supporting a column on which an arch marking this division may have sprung. In total the structure may have been nearly 50m wide and at least 80-100m long. Excavations showed that its floor was covered with a fine floor of reused tiles and thin stone slabs. Hints at a lavish interior come from a small number of marble fragments of pieces of window glass, although they were all from secondary contexts.

This large structure was clearly of great importance, even though its actual surviving remains were so slight. There are no finds from the building which explicitly suggest that it was the remains of a church. However, the excavators

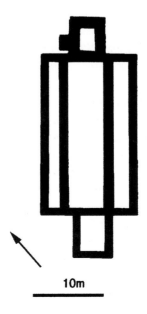

10m

16 *Basilica structure from Insula XI,* Verulamium *(St Albans)*

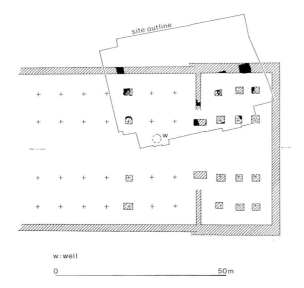

17 *Large basilica from Colchester House, London. It bears similarities in plan to the church of St Tecla in Milan.* Sankey, 1998

w:well

0   50m

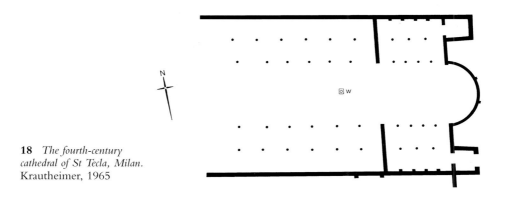

18 *The fourth-century cathedral of St Tecla, Milan.* Krautheimer, 1965

have drawn attention to the close parallels between the Colchester House building and the remains of the late fourth-century cathedral of St Tecla from Milan (**18**). A comparison of the plans of the two buildings shows a clear resemblance, though there are slight differences such as the additional post-pad supporting the putative sanctuary arch. Similar supporting columns are, however, known from other late fourth- and early fifth-century churches, such as St Giovanni Evangelista in Ravenna. Despite these parallels with churches, the identification of this building as a church is still tentative. Other suggestions for its function include a *horreum*, a large state-built granary used for the collection of *annona*, the late Roman tax in kind, or a treasury. London, with its prime position in the governance of the provinces would have undoubtedly had an important church, though the jury is still out as to whether this was one of them. If it was a church, its size and its parallels with St Tecla's, a possible imperial foundation in an imperial capital, would imply it was a large and extremely important one. Although it stood away from the centre of the town, (London's main forum-basilica) which was a common site for the construction of cathedrals elsewhere in the Empire, was razed to the ground in the early fourth century, and the land left was an open space. Whatever the reason for the levelling of this central area of the town, it may suggest a slight rearrangement of the internal topography of the capital with a shift in the focus of power in the town to the south-east of the enceinte. Certainly the defences in the area were supplemented in the fourth century; a number of bastions were added to the east side of the town wall *c.*351-75 and a second phase of a defensive wall along the river *c.*390. The cemeteries to the east of Roman London also continued to be used into the early fifth century, perhaps also implying a continued vitality in this part of the capital. However, even if this tentative and circumstantial evidence for a subtle shift of focus within late Roman London is correct, it does not necessarily support the identification of the Colchester House building as a church, as the other identifications of the structure as a granary or treasury would be equally at home in this context.

If this basilica was not the site of London's church then what are the alternatives? Few locations suggest themselves with any degree of credibility. Most of the evidence is negative; the levelling of the forum-basilica makes a central cathedral with its associated structures unlikely in this area. Another possible site for a church is in the south-west of the town, in the area of St Paul's Cathedral. Bede recorded that this was the site of the first Anglo-Saxon bishopric in England, dating to AD 604. However, this is based purely on a speculative assumption of continuity of worship on this important site, for which there is no material evidence. Although the lack of hard evidence for a Roman church from London is a little surprising, it need not be of great concern. A Christian church is just one of the important buildings from Late Roman London which we have good reason to believe existed, such as the headquarters of the *vicarius* of Britain, the imperial treasury and probably the consular governor of Maxima Caesariensis. The possible absence of the remains of a cathedral, as well as these other buildings, says more about the poor preservation of the Roman remains beneath the cellars of London than the presence or absence of Christianity.

Churches outside town walls

If the evidence for churches inside city walls is small, there is slightly more evidence for possible church structures in suburban areas. Perhaps the best surviving example of a suburban church from Roman Britain is that which stands just on the north-west edge of the late Roman cemetery at Butt Road outside the Roman city of *Camulodunum* (Colchester). This building had been recognised as early as 1845, and the first recorded excavation took place in the 1930s. It was subsequently re-excavated in the 1978-9 and 1988 by the Colchester Archaeological Trust.

The walls of the building were made of stone, and the roof was probably covered with typical Roman ceramic tiles. Within the structure evidence for floors is minimal, no tiles or tesserae were found and a simple sand or earth floor is most likely. Despite the simple floors, other aspects of the building may have been more lavish; fragments of painted wall plaster were found, as were fragments of a thin slab of marble, which probably formed a veneer decoration. At the west end was an apse. The excavators argued that this was a later addition, though the phasing is not clear on this point and it may have been an original design feature. Equally unclear is the exact chronological position of a series of post-holes separating a north and a south aisle from the central nave. Again, the excavators argue that these belong to a secondary phase of development, though if they had any structural role it would seem more likely that they were part of the building as originally planned. Nine metres from the east end was a number of smaller post-holes which may have marked a cross-screen. Many of the features from the church were filled with soil containing large quantities of animal bone and Roman coins.

Before the building had been constructed there was a single grave on the site. This seems to have had an unusual wooden vault or superstructure. When the basilica was built it was aligned on this grave, which was positioned just in front of the apse. This was later cut by one or possibly two secondary graves. At a late date in the period of using the church, a pit was dug close to the apse. It contained an array of unusual objects including a silver armlet and ring, several iron objects, painted plaster and marble as well as part of a human skull and thigh bone. A hoard of at least 186 coins was also found. The latest coins from this group dated to the early fifth century. The pit was sealed with a large slab of worked stone, probably architectural in origin. To the west of the structure, a second, smaller building stood. This surrounded a substantial tile structure around 1.1m by 1.3m and was made up of at least three layers of broken tile set in daub. This was interpreted as a hearth, and the structure was probably associated with the cooking of funerary feasts.

Once again, the identification of this building as a church is not certain. This partly revolves around the date of construction. The excavators state that at the earliest it was constructed in the mid-third century, but believe it is most likely to have been built between 320 and 340 and was related to a sudden increase in coin loss in this period. Martin Millett in his detailed critique of the excavator's report has pointed out that these coins were not stratified beneath the structure and do not give a strict *terminus post quem*. Their use as dating evidence for the building is purely circumstantial. Millett interprets the structure as a hall used for the feasting, as indicated by the animal and bird bones, related to pagan funerary rites associated with the adjacent cemetery, and he argues that the structure was built sometime after *c*.AD 294. However, as Millett himself admits there are no parallels for such an apsidal funerary hall from Britain. He puts this down to the lack of excavated cemetery sites in Roman Britain, though his characterisation of the state of Roman funerary studies is perhaps overly negative and no such funerary halls have emerged in the publications of Roman cemeteries since his review.

Paradoxically, the most likely example of the site of a Roman church is also the most elusive. As we have seen, the presence of a martyrium at *Verulamium* was well attested in the early medieval period. It is virtually certain that such a memorial church would have been sited on the real or believed grave of St Alban. Whatever the precise date of Alban's death, his grave would have been in one of the cemeteries surrounding the walled area of the Roman city. Significantly, the site of the present cathedral in the city has also been shown by excavation to be located on the site of a late Roman cemetery. Martin Biddle's excavations revealed over 50 Roman graves to the south of the present, medieval structure and another 27 to the north. Curiously, many of these graves were sealed by a gravelled surface probably laid down in the late fourth century. Many finds were associated with this layer, including over 100 coins dating as late as the early fifth century and many fragments of pottery and glassware. This assemblage was not typical, as the proportion of glass fragments to pottery fragments was abnormally high, making it unlikely to be the remains of normal domestic activity. The gravel layer was deposited at the same time or slightly earlier than two large north-south ditches dug to the east of these burials. Although, there is absolutely no evidence for a late Roman church structure, the presence of a late Roman cemetery followed by indications that in the late fourth century the site developed in a curious, but not fully understood way, combined with the later presence of an Anglo-Saxon and medieval cathedral is highly suggestive. However, this site is not the only possible extramural church from *Verulamium*. In another cemetery, known as Verulam Hills Fields, to the south of the town a flint-walled basilical structure was excavated in the early 1960s.

Rural churches

The evidence for rural churches in Britain is as sparse as that for urban churches. The situation is complicated by the fact that the slight evidence we do have suggests that the basilical form was not used. Instead, the few possible examples seem to indicate that simple rectangular structures were used.

The best example of this is the small church found at Icklingham, Suffolk (**19**). The circumstantial evidence suggests that this site may have been of some religious importance before the mid-fourth century when much of the site was

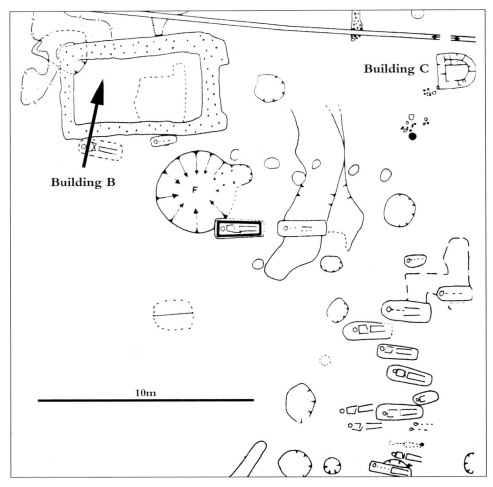

19 *Possible church (building B) from Icklingham (Suffolk). Building C to its west is probably a font base or baptistery*

covered by a layer of chalk around 25cm thick. The foundations of a small rectangular building, measuring 7.4m by 4.6m, were cut into this layer. Little evidence of the superstructure of this building survived, though enough could be seen to suggest that the walls were mainly built of mortared flints. Surrounding the building were over forty burials with their heads to the west. Only one contained any grave-goods, a small pile of bracelets at the foot of the grave. To the east of the rectangular building was a small apsidal structure, which appeared to be a tank or cistern; this is likely to have been a small baptismal font. However, even with the presence of the font, the Christian nature of the site would be apparent due to the discovery of two lead tanks bearing Christian *chi-rho* symbols to the north of the same field. Another similar tank had previously been found *c.*1725 in the same general area. As will

be seen later, the area around Icklingham appears to have been a focus for
votive offerings of both a Christian and pagan nature, and the site is unique in
the presence of a probable church, font, burials and clearly Christian objects.
Importantly, there are no elements of the rectangular building that are diagnostically Christian, and in a different context a religious purpose for it would
not have been suggested.

It has been suggested that there may have been a small pagan religious site
preceding the Christian activity at Icklingham. There are a few other
examples of small rectangular buildings being found adjacent to disused
Roman pagan temples. At Lamyatt Beacon, in Somerset, a small Roman
temple of typical Romano-British form stood on the summit of the hill. Just
to the north of the temple stood a small rectangular building (c.4.5m by 3m)
aligned west-east (**20A**). It had stone walls made from mortared limestone,
and was floored with limestone paving slabs. Inside were traces of internal
stone benches offset from the inside faces of the walls. These benches were
found along the north, west and south walls. The entrance to the structure
was presumably along the less well-recorded east wall. The date of the
construction of the building is unclear, beyond the fact that it post-dated the
late third century. To the north of the structure at least sixteen burials were
found. These were laid in a west-east direction, with no grave-goods.
However, these graves were dated by carbon 14 to the sixth and seventh
centuries AD, significantly post-dating the Roman period.

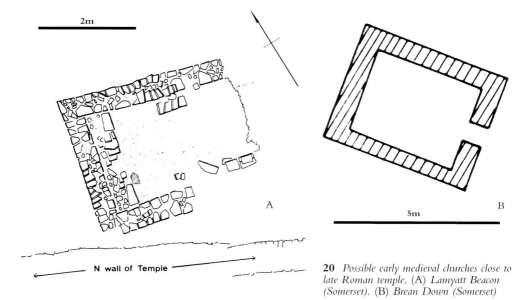

2m

A

5m

B

N wall of Temple

20 *Possible early medieval churches close to
late Roman temple.* (A) *Lamyatt Beacon
(Somerset).* (B) *Brean Down (Somerset)*

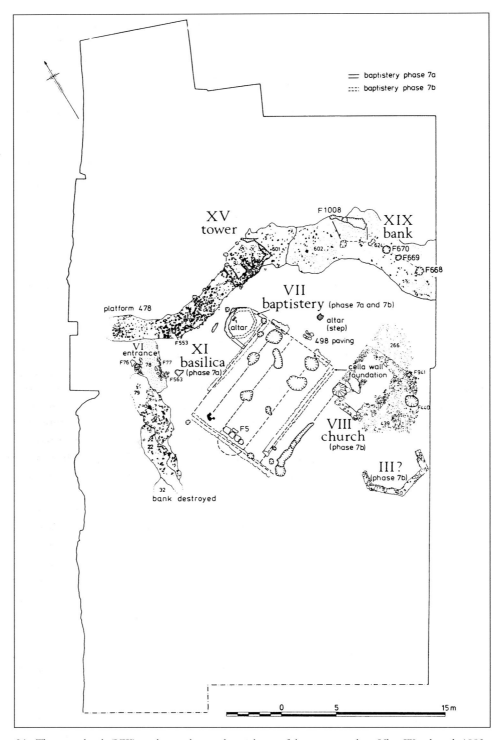

21 *The stone church (VIII) can be seen here to the south-east of the pagan temple at Uley.* Woodward, 1993

A very similar situation occurs at Brean Down, a small peninsula jutting out into the Bristol Channel. Here, another small Romano-British style pagan temple was built. It was probably demolished c.AD 390. Once more a small rectangular building was then built (**20B**). It was similar in size to the Lamyatt Beacon structure, and was also aligned west-east. It too had three internal stone benches. A small early medieval cemetery was laid out around the site. In places, graves overlay parts of the demolished temple, but did not cut into the rectangular structure.

A third rectangular stone structure next to a disused Roman temple can be found at Uley (Glos.). This was the site of a large religious complex, which had a substantial temple, as well as a number of other associated structures. After the collapse of the temple, and partly overlying the debris, was a small (5.5m by 4.25m) rectangular building aligned roughly south-west to north-east (**21**). The foundations indicate that it had limestone walls and a well-laid limestone floor. Unlike the other structures it had a small rectangular apse to the south-west. The entrance was presumably in the north-east end of the building, which was surrounded externally by an area of cobbling.

Although all these buildings clearly post-date the Roman temples next to which they were built, it is not clear whether they date to the late Roman period or not. The buildings at Lamyatt Beacon and Brean Down are both associated with early medieval cemeteries, and it is equally possible that they are more related to the fifth to seventh centuries. The excavators of Uley also placed the rectangular structure there in the sixth century. The internal benches found at Lamyatt Beacon and Brean Down are also features found only in small early medieval churches such as that from the hermitage site at St Helen's in the Isles of Scilly and the similar site of Ardwall Island (Dumfries and Galloway) (**22**). These buildings may have been built on Roman sites and bear a superficial resemblance to the Icklingham church, however they are more at home in the fifth to seventh century rather than the Roman period.

A final possible, and more unusual, example of a possible Roman church comes from the Roman religious site of Nettleton (Wilts.). Like Uley, the central building of this site was a Romano-British temple surrounded by a complex of subsidiary buildings. Towards the end of the first half of the fourth century the octagonal temple saw a phase of major alteration (**23**). The internal organisation of the building was rearranged. Previously the building had contained a series of radial walls forming eight large niches centred on a central room. With the addition of a number of small walls four of the niches were blocked off. The external entrances of the building were also blocked leaving only an eastern entrance. The internal walls of the structure were decorated with plaster that had an X-shaped design with a central roundel painted on it. However, the precise layout of the building is still not entirely understood, as the chambers blocked off by the new walls were also internally decorated with plaster decoration, which would be unusual if they were entirely blocked from

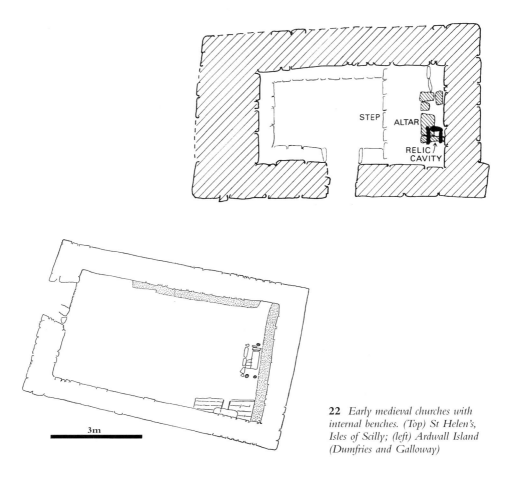

3m

22 *Early medieval churches with internal benches. (Top) St Helen's, Isles of Scilly; (left) Ardwall Island (Dumfries and Galloway)*

view. These changes created a cruciform-shaped internal space within the building. It has been suggested by the excavator that this was intentional and the building was being reused as a church. Although unknown elsewhere in Britain there are parallels for quatrefoil and octagonal churches elsewhere in the Roman Empire, such as the martyrium of St Phillip at Hieropolis (Pamukkale, Turkey), the Mausoleum of Galla Placidia (Ravenna, Italy), the church of San Lorenzo (Milan, Italy) and the so-called 'Golden Octagon' (Antioch, Turkey). However, most of these are built on a vastly larger scale. This is partly because they are all heavily influenced by Roman Imperial church design, particularly the 'Golden Octagon' begun by Constantine in 327 and completed by 341. This was the earliest example of such a church, and the other examples date to the late fourth or fifth century AD. It seems unlikely that a small church in Western Britain should be taking on the architectural innovations being developed in the Eastern Empire on such a reduced scale at such an early date. The structural alterations at Nettleton may have more

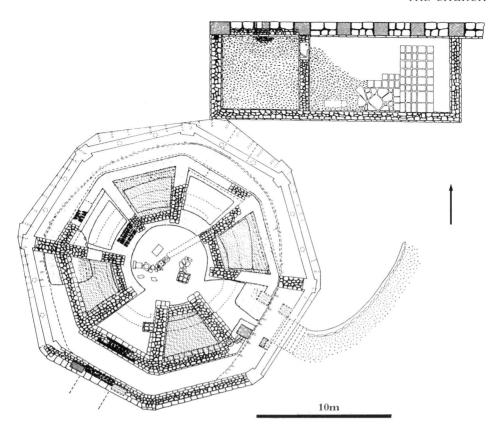

23 *The octagonal pagan temple at Nettleton Shrubs, Wiltshire.* Wedlake, 1982

practical motivations. The temple had been struck by problems with subsidence. These changes to the internal plan of the building may have had more to do with the practical need to keep the building upright, than a change in religious affiliation.

A final, small group of rural structures which have had a Christian function attributed to them are the small two-roomed structures found at Witham (Building F4044), Maiden Castle and Nettleton (Building 23) (**24**). These structures vary slightly in size. Unlike the other structures discussed so far they are made up of two almost equal sized rooms. However, these rooms appear to have been the result of a secondary phase of expansion. The structure at Witham was originally 3.0m by 3.0m; the addition of an extra room increased it in size to 3.0m by 5.0m. The second room was added to the south, giving the completed structure a north-south alignment. It is not clear where the external entrance was, but there was a door between the two chambers. This differs from the larger Maiden Castle and Nettleton structures. The roughly

73

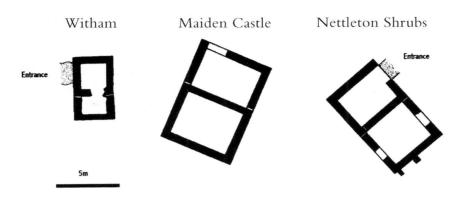

24 *Two-roomed structures from late Roman religious sites*

west-east aligned primary structure (5.8m by 4.5m) north of the Romano-British temple at Maiden Castle has an additional chamber added to the north giving the new structure (8.2m by 5.8m) a north-south alignment. There was no sign of a door between the two buildings, though there was a door in the north wall of the primary element. At Nettleton, Building 23, which stood close to a group of presumed late Roman burials, had an initial phase (4.8m by 3.9m) with a door in the eastern wall, followed by the addition of a second room to the south creating a larger building (7.9m by 4.8m). This second room had doors in the east and west walls. There is little evidence for the use of any of these buildings, except at Nettleton where there was a row of possible hearths along the north wall of the primary room. This suggests it may have been related to the preparation of funerary feasts related to the nearby cemetery. The reasons for a suggestion of a possible Christian function are unclear – the Witham example may have been called a church because of the presence of a nearby baptistery, and the assumption that this required an associated church. The Nettleton example may have been given a possible Christian identity on the basis of its closeness to a cemetery and the believed Christian nature of the altered late Roman temple nearby (see above). The Maiden Castle structure may have been called Christian merely because of its parallels with the other two buildings. In reality, there is nothing in the nature of the buildings which implies that they were a church. Whilst the simple primary phases from Maiden Castle and Witham may have some similarities with the buildings at Lamyatt Beacon and Brean Down, the addition of the extra rooms is not paralleled elsewhere. In any case the buildings at Lamyatt Beacon and Brean Down are more likely to be early medieval in date.

This brings us to one of the problems in recognising rural churches. The structure from Icklingham, which is the structure with the best case for being a Roman church is a simple rectangular building. If it had been found without the nearby lead tanks it would not have been recognised as a church. Simple rectangular buildings abound on rural sites in Britain. Undoubtedly, with the huge majority of these simple domestic or agricultural structures, the fundamental problem is that there is no way of recognising the tiny minority which might be churches. There was nothing inherent in the plan or structure of these possible rural churches that distinguished them from secular buildings.

Military

A final assemblage of possible churches are a group of structures from military sites. This intriguing group has produced some of the best evidence for Christian buildings in Britain. One of the first to be excavated was that which stood within the walls of the important fort at Richborough (Kent), in the far south-east corner of Britain. The possible church stood in the north-east corner of the fort (**25**). Unfortunately the excavation that revealed this structure took place in 1923 and the techniques used were not as sophisticated as would have been used to examine a similar site today. The top 0.9m of the topsoil at the site was removed in bulk in preparation for examining the lower levels of the Roman military occupation. This was the practice at the time, when there was a tendency to begin excavation at the first levels of masonry, and no consideration was given to the survival of more fragile deposits above. Site photographs, however, showed a number of stone blocks found during this phase. These blocks formed two lines at right-angles to each other. These blocks seem to suggest a roughly west-east aligned rectangular structure supported by wooden timbers standing on stone post-pads. The sparse remains of the structure give us little other information about the site, though it seems to have dated to the late fourth century. There would be nothing to suggest that this building's structure was a church if it were not for the presence of an almost certain masonry font just to the north of the building (see chapter 4).

Richborough is not the only fort to contain possible evidence for a Christian church. A number of Roman military sites along Hadrian's Wall have produced evidence for apsidal structures which may be interpreted as churches. The best candidate for a church is the recently discovered structure at Vindolanda, where the possible church lay in the southern section of the *praetorium* courtyard (**26**). Its stone foundations were laid over the flagstones of the yard. In places, a number of smaller stones were laid on these larger stones to create a level surface, possibly for wooden beams. At the western end was a small apse about 4m wide, the east end of the structure joined the wall of the yard. The precise date of the building is uncertain; though it is clear it was built some time after the abandonment of the courtyard, as there was at least 0.2m

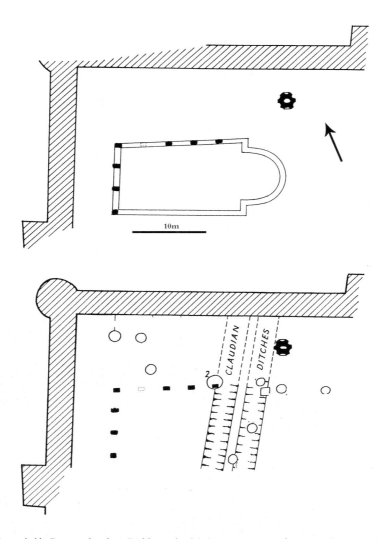

25 *The probable Roman church at Richborough. (Top), interpretation of remains, (bottom), plan of remains discovered by Brown*

of build-up between the floor of the yard and the church. The excavators have suggested a construction date sometime around AD 400 or a little later.

Another apsidal structure has been revealed at the nearby fort at Housesteads (**27**). This building lies to the north–west of the fort. It was found during excavations in 1898, so many details of the site are unclear. However, it appears to have been a rectangular building with an apsidal west end. It was not completely uncovered, but appears to be at least 6m by 10m. Its precise date is unclear, though it is likely to date to the late fourth century or later. Interestingly, a possible long-cist burial or cistern has been found to the north-west of this structure, though again its date is open.

26 *Possible church at Vindolanda*

27 *Possible church at Housesteads uncovered during R.C. Bosanquet's late nineteenth-century excavations.* Copyright The Museum of Antiquities of the Society of Antiquities, Newcastle upon Tyne

A likely Roman church has also been found in the fort at South Shields. It was built on the site of the *principia*, the headquarters building of the fort (**28**). The most striking aspect of this structure was the presence of a possible stone altar, probably of Christian rather than pagan origin. This altar appears to have been surrounded on three sides by a stone structure, which may have been a rectangular, eastern apse for a rectangular stone building. It is probable that the northern wall of the church was formed by a surviving wall from an earlier building on the site. This would give the structure a probable internal width of around 9.4m and a length of *c.*13m. The west end of the church may have been attached to parts of a colonnade, which surrounded the courtyard in

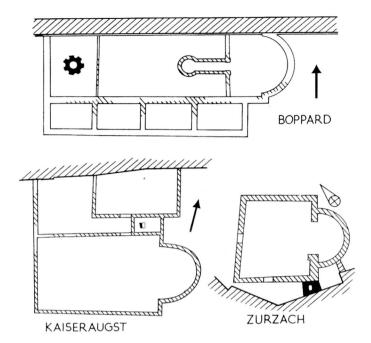

28 *Late Roman churches from Roman forts in Germany.* Brown 1971

which the church stood. This may have acted as a simple narthex or entrance area. The north wall appears to have fallen inwards sometime in the fifth or sixth century. Its surviving remains show that it may have been over 9m tall. It appears that a door was cut through the wall, though it is not clear whether this was used whilst the probable church was in use. The precise date of construction of this structure is unclear, though a broad late fourth-century date is most likely.

The presence of churches on military sites should not be a surprise. Similar structures are known from forts, which were part of the military frontiers along the Rhine-Danube frontier. For example, a church has been found at Boppard (Germany) on the south bank of the Rhine. This building, with an apse at the east end contained the remains of a seven-sided font in the western narthex. Its construction is dated to the early fifth century.

House churches

So far the focus has been on what might be termed 'public' churches. However, in the late Roman period there was another category of church, often known as the 'house church'. Put simply, these small chapels were located inside private houses. Most of the earliest Christian churches would probably have existed along these lines. In times of persecution the decision to hold the mass in domestic buildings was driven primarily by the need for secrecy. The legal inability of the pre-AD 313 church to hold property as a corporate body would also have forced many congregations to worship in properties owned by one of its members. These earliest of churches would have shown little evidence for any architectural elaboration or decoration, and may well have had other functions when not being used for worship. However, in some areas where the community felt some level of security they may have felt able to adorn the chapel in an overtly Christian manner. The best example of this comes from the far eastern edge of the Roman Empire at the border town of Dura Europos (Syria), where the filling in of a series of rooms to help buttress defences led to the chance preservation of a Synagogue, a Mithraeum and a Christian house-church with a baptistery. All three retained well-preserved painted murals. Although those from the mid third-century house church were cruder than those from the other two religious buildings they could be clearly seen to represent a series of scenes from the scripture. Images in the baptistery could be recognised as scenes such as David and Goliath, Jesus walking on the waves and the Good Shepherd. The few others that are known were incorporated into the later structure of a church. For example, parts of a shop and one or two upper rooms are embedded into the later fabric of the church of SS. Giovanni e Paolo in Rome. Even here, early Christian use would not have been certain if it had not been for the surviving wall painting of a figure in praying position from *c.*AD 250. Not surprisingly, there are no clear examples of such a house church used by an underground congregation from Roman Britain.

The notion of the house church did not end once Christianity became a *religio licita*, though it is likely their mode of use did. The one certain example of a house church from Britain comes from the villa at Lullingstone (Kent), one of a series of wealthy villas that were built along the valley of the River Darent. The villa itself was first built in the late first century AD, but the evidence for Christianity, unsurprisingly, only first appears in the mid- to late fourth century. The evidence for the house church survived in the form of the reconstructed scheme of wall paintings from an upstairs room. It was only due to the meticulous excavation of the site that this was possible, and it was the first time that such plaster had been carefully conserved in Britain. In an ante-room to the main chamber a large *chi-rho* symbol, flanked by an alpha and omega, was painted on the wall (**29**). The west wall of the main room was decorated with a series of figures in the *orantes* pose, the typically early Christian prayer position (**30**). A second *chi-rho* symbol was painted on the south wall, as well as several more possible figures, though they are not so well understood. On the north wall more figures were painted, and it appears to have shown buildings, as well as vegetal motifs and at least one animal, probably a dog. The fragmentary

29 *Wall painting from the Roman villa at Lullingstone (Kent) showing a frieze of praying figures*

30 *Painted* chi-rho *symbol from the Roman villa at Lullingstone (Kent).* Copyright British Museum

nature of this scene makes it difficult to interpret, but it may have shown a scriptural scene. Finally, on the east wall, yet another *chi-rho* was shown, as well as traces of more figures. This small group of rooms, a porch, the ante-room and the main church chamber had previously been integrated into the main house structure, but, at the same time as murals were painted, the access routes were changed and the suite could only be entered from an outside door. These rooms clearly do not conform to the typical basilical church plan, but in some ways there are still some parallels. For example, the ante-room may have acted as a *narthex*. It is not clear though, which wall would have been the focus of worship.

Lullingstone is not the only late Roman villa with Christian imagery in its rooms. A number of villas from south-west Britain have mosaic pavements with Christian imagery. At Hinton St Mary (Dorset) the central roundel of one pavement shows a head with a *chi-rho* symbol behind it; this is almost certainly a representation of Jesus (**31**). Nearby, at Frampton a large mosaic depicts the image of the classical hero Bellerophon battling the Chimaera, but to one side is an apse decorated with another *chi-rho* symbol. Is it possible that these are churches? Certainly the plan of the rooms from Frampton recall that of a basilica, with an apse and a *narthex* (**32**). However, unlike the

31 *Probable head of Christ from the fourth-century mosaic at Hinton St Mary (Dorset).*
Copyright British Museum

32 *Plan of possible house church at Frampton*

Christian rooms from Lullingstone, these rooms appear to be integrated into the main villa building, and the Hinton St Mary pavement appears to have come from the central reception of the building. It seems unlikely that such a main room in a villa, which would usually have been used for the reception of guests, would have been given over entirely to Christian worship. As we shall see later, such overt Christian imagery would be just as much at home in such an audience chamber as in a church. At Frampton, despite the architectural echoes of a church structure it is also unlikely that the room acted primarily as a church or chapel, as the Christian image is sited next to the pagan Bellerophon scene. Again, as we shall see later, the juxtaposition of pagan and Christian motifs is not uncommon in secular spaces or on objects. However, the intrusion of pagan motifs into the decorative scheme of a church is unknown. Whilst both these rooms are unlikely to have been churches in which mass was celebrated, they may have had other quasi-religious functions on occasions. For example, the occupants of the villa may have gathered together for prayers here or they may have at times acted as a more private oratory.

What is clear from the evidence for house churches in Britain and elsewhere is that like other types of church they are very hard to recognise. If it had not been for the fortuitous survival of the decorative wall paintings at both Lullingstone and Dura Europos, neither structure would have been identified as being a church. Evidence from writers such as Sidonius

Apollinaris (fifth century) and Ausonius (fourth century) makes it clear that house churches existed in Gaul, yet archaeological evidence for them is sparse. At sites such as Beaucaire (Gers) amongst others, the evidence for Christian activity at the site is only recognisable in the fifth century when a cemetery grew up on the site.

Forms

In a period when a standard architectural form for the church was only slowly being put together it is not surprising that the plans of possible Romano-British churches show wide variation. Although most are broadly basilical in plan the biggest variation is in the nature of the apse. Most have the typical eastern apse, though some structures, such as the Silchester building, have a western apse. In some cases, the apse springs either straight from the end of the building, such as Vindolanda, or with only a slight return, such as St Paul-in-the-Bail (Lincoln) or Icklingham. However, in buildings with aisles, the apse usually springs from the end of the chancel, as can be seen at Butt Road, Colchester or Silchester. The apse was usually used to emphasise the location of the altar. The precise location of altars in Romano-British churches is rarely clear. The position of a probable altar can be seen at Silchester, marked by a small mosaic panel. This was sited just within the main building in front of the apse. However, the only example of an actual altar from one of the buildings discussed above actually stands within the apse itself. The altar from South Shields consisted of a simple stone shaft supporting a stone table-like slab. This is exceptionally unusual, and altars of this date are rare in all parts of the Roman Empire. It was distinctly different in shape to the typical pagan altar, which usually consisted of a rectangular monolithic block. Their functions, of course, were very different. The pagan altars were used primarily as supports for sacrifices, both of animals and other foodstuffs. In contrast, Christian altars were used to celebrate the Eucharist, which did not include any sacrifices; instead liturgical objects and the church plate may have been placed on them. However, Christian altars at this time did not have to be made from stone, and a wooden table may have sufficed. The possibility of portable altars must also be considered. These are mentioned in sixth-century sources from Brittany; the same text also states that these were used to celebrate mass in houses, doing away with the need for any church structure at all.

There is evidence for a range of internal divisions within these buildings. The best-preserved examples can be seen at Silchester, where there are two clearly defined aisles with transeptal spaces, and a clearly defined narthex. A possible narthex is to be found at Colchester, where there is a division across the nave of the basilica. It is possible that the west end of the churches at St

Paul-in-the-Bail and South Shields abutted the porticos of the courtyards within which they were placed. These may have formed small narthex-like lobbies, as may the anteroom at Lullingstone.

Although it is possible to draw some conclusions about the plan of these early churches it is more difficult to get a better understanding of their super-structures. There are hints that some of the earlier churches may have been extensively decorated. In a fifth-century description of a church in Lyons the writer Sidonius Appollinaris mentions a gilded ceiling, marble columns and floors and green glass windows. Fragments of marble veneer have been found at the London Colchester House basilica, Flaxengate (Lincoln) and Butt Road (Colchester). These may have been part of an elaborate scheme of decoration; these are most likely to have been abstract and geometric, such as was increas-ingly common in fifth-century churches such as the church of Santa Sabina (Rome), though complex figurative designs are also known. The remains of the decorative scheme of murals from Lullingstone are also clear indicators that many churches may have contained painted plasterwork. Fragments of painted plaster have been found at Flaxengate (Lincoln) and Butt Road (Colchester). Although not from a church, probable Christian painted plaster has also been found from the small mausoleum at the cemetery of Poundbury.

It is quite likely that the churches contained other forms of decoration, which may not have survived in the archaeological record. Curtains and hangings may have been used to section off areas of the church, such as the narthex and the aisles. It is also probable that woodwork, such as the coffered ceilings that were common in basilicas, would have been painted.

The way in which these buildings were lit is unclear. Where the building had aisles the main windows are likely to have been formed part of a clerestory, where the sloped roof over the aisles met the body of the main church, running above an arcade. No clear examples of window glass have been found from any of these churches, but it is likely they may have been blocked by thin layers of horn or mica or simply left open. Internal lighting would probably have been provided by lamps, rather than candles. Five simple ceramic oil lamps were found at the site of the Butt Road church. More elaborate hanging lamps may also have been used. It is possible that the hanging-bowls, which were included in the Water Newton treasure may have had such a purpose, and fragments of possible glass lamps have been found at Lullingstone.

Conclusions

The evidence from Britain has shown the remains of a number of possible and probable churches, ranging from the potential cathedral in London to the more typical small urban churches, such as Silchester and Butt Road, Colchester. Whilst the total of likely churches is not large, the spread is not dissimilar from northern Gaul. The elaborate baptisteries and large church complexes which are often discussed when exploring Late Antique Christianity in Gaul are virtually all fifth-century or later. Churches of the fourth century are rare in the northern provinces of Lugdunensis (Senona, Secunda and Tertia) and Belgica (Prima and Secunda). In many areas of the Roman Empire these early fourth-century churches are usually only identifiable as Christian structures due to the continuity of worship in the site leaving the standing structures or remains of definite churches. If only the fourth-century levels of these structures were discovered the debate over their identification would be as intense as that over the possible Romano-British churches discussed above.

Another problem with recognising fourth-century Roman churches in Britain is the same that applies to any investigation of late Roman structures in the area: the difficulty of recognising wooden structures. Although some of the earlier churches discussed above, such as Silchester, were built of brick or stone, many of the later ones appear to have been built partially or totally of wood. The presence of post-pads at Richborough suggests that the main superstructure of the building was supported on wooden posts. The early churches at St Paul-in-the-Bail were also probably made of timber; there is no evidence to suggest that the trenches had once contained stone foundations. The churches from the northern frontier are also likely to have been built primarily from wood. Although the simple, shallow foundations of the church at Vindolanda was made from stone, it had been carefully levelled to support timber sill-beams rather than a stone superstructure. These examples all seem to belong to the later fourth or fifth century, whereas the mid-fourth-century buildings, such as Silchester and Butt Road, Colchester, appear to be more substantial structures. This appears to reflect a wider late fourth-century phenomenon in Roman Britain. There was a decrease in the construction of new masonry structures and there was a wider movement towards the use of timber structures. This has implications for the recognition of possible late Roman churches. It is much harder to recognise the archaeological remains of simple timber structures than substantial masonry buildings. This is particularly true of later Roman structures, which are stratigraphically and physically higher than other Roman remains. They are thus more susceptible to damage by post-Roman events, ranging from Anglo-Saxon graves to Victorian cellars. It is only in the last 50 years that archaeologists have become increasingly aware of the possibility of recovering these more fragile remains. Before World War Two there was a tendency for excavators to ignore the apparently barren late Roman levels; instead they dug down to the better-preserved earlier levels, destroying the more ephemeral later fourth and fifth century remains.

Clearly, although Roman Britain was not lavishly provided with churches, it was not significantly different from northern Gaul. The contrast between Britain and other parts of the Late Antique road only becomes really marked in the fifth and sixth centuries. Even this contrast was probably not so much in numbers, but in style; whilst European church building continued to be primarily in stone, churches in Britain appeared to have been built primarily in wood, a tendency already beginning in the late fourth century.

4

BECOMING CHRISTIAN

Most people are born into their religion. In traditional societies children follow the religious practices of their parents, even if in later life they choose a different path. Amongst the pagan religions of the Roman Empire, there was no sense that worshipping a new god meant rejecting others. Worshippers undoubtedly had personal favourite gods and identified with others through tribal, regional or occupational loyalties, but they did not spurn other deities. Instead there was a widespread tolerance of religious belief. Persecution against Christians and even the execution of Jesus was driven more by the political implications of their beliefs than any sense of theological dogma. However, a small number of religions such as Judaism and Christianity required their worshippers to reject all other divinities as false gods, holding that they alone provided the correct path to salvation. The decision to become a Christian did not just mean 'bolting on' Jesus and God to a pre-existing pantheon of gods. Instead, the convert was required to actively reject earlier beliefs. In a society in which loyalty to certain gods and participation in religious ceremonies were important aspects of daily life, and formed part of the social glue which held communities together, the rejection of these gods had fundamental social implications. This made the job of Christian evangelists so much more challenging. They were not just preaching religious change; they were trying to persuade potential converts to alter their relationship to the societies in which they lived as well as their relationship to the gods.

Although in its earliest days Christianity was essentially a reform sect of Judaism it soon developed a missionary drive to make converts from non-Jews. Whilst the early evangelists may have wished to bring people of all ranks and beliefs into the fold of the Church it was inevitable that certain sections of the community showed a greater tendency to convert than others. A wide range of factors would have influenced which group within a partic-ular society would have been most likely to switch religion. Initially the most important factor would be whether the potential convert was physically in the right location to hear about the new religion. Despite the constant letter writing of the early disciples, the vast majority of religious teaching would have taken place through face-to-face encounters between the preacher and his audience. As a persecuted religion the opportunity for public preaching would have been limited; this would immediately influence the sections of the community who may have considered converting.

The first Christian communities in the Empire appear to have developed in certain specific contexts. Most obviously, the majority of early converts appear to have been located within cities rather than in rural areas. Although the majority of the population of the Roman Empire were country dwellers, the cities formed crucial focal points for the administrative and communication networks. The size of the population in these towns would have given the earliest preachers the chance to reach decent size audiences, as well as the protection that large numbers bring in times of persecution. The cosmopolitan nature of the larger cities of the Roman Empire provided other supportive factors. The Jewish community was greatly involved in trade and small communities of Jews were found in most of the large trading cities of the Empire, though they were more common in the east. These small communities would have been useful for Christian missionaries, particularly if they were of Jewish background themselves. They would provide a group of potential converts already open to the concept of monotheism, and with an understanding of the historical and religious issues that Christianity was trying to engage with. The wider network of kinship and alliances commonly found amongst merchant communities may also have provided more practical support and access to local society. The evidence for Judaism in Roman Britain is almost entirely absent, though it is intriguing that the name of one of the martyrs of Caerleon, Aaron, may suggest a Jewish background. Whilst it is likely that London may have housed a small group of Jewish traders there is, as yet, no hard evidence.

The lack of any definite evidence for Christianity in Britain from before the freedom of the church in the early fourth century makes it difficult to draw any conclusions about which groups were the first to convert. The limited historical records we have preserve no complex narratives of the process of conversion, and as we have seen the earliest are based on fundamental errors in the understanding of these events. The fundamental change in the religious balance of power caused by Constantine's conversion makes it dangerous to extrapolate patterns of conversion back into the earlier period. However, it is possible to draw broad inferences from what we know about the process elsewhere in the Empire where we have better information.

From the very beginning when Jesus chose his disciples Christianity seems to have first attracted lower and middle status individuals rather than the upper classes. This may have been for a range of reasons. Perhaps most important was Christianity's emphasis on salvation in the hereafter. Rather than emphasising short-term solutions to day-to-day difficulties it offered instead a more profound reward after death. It also linked the chances of obtaining this reward to faith rather than simply performing the correct rituals. At a time when religious observance appears to have been often linked to ostentatious sacrifices and donations to temples, this early form of Christianity must have appealed to those with little economic freedom. It was amongst this group that the notion of salvation would also have appealed. To those with little personal control over their day-to-day lives, the Church offered the chance to exercise personal control over their greater destinies. When pagan writers mocked early Christianity as appealing only to slaves, children and women, this may not have merely been a joke. It was amongst these sectors of society that such a religion might have been most influential.

However, Christianity did not only have something to offer the least powerful in society. The church may have given the middling sort an opportunity to opt out of social arenas dominated by the wealthier elites, such as civic giving or the support of pagan religious ceremonies. Instead by opting into a smaller religious community they may have been able to extricate themselves from these networks, and instead embed themselves into new communities, becoming 'big fish in small ponds'.

It is important to remember that for the vast majority of converts, particularly in times of persecution, the decision to convert must have been a difficult and profound one. Many will have converted out of a genuine change in religious belief. However, whilst the factors considered above may not have been linked explicitly to the decision to change religions, they would undoubtedly have had a profound, and doubtlessly subconscious, effect on the underlying thought processes behind the conversion.

Inevitably with the conversion of Constantine, the Church found itself moving in the prevailing religious current. For the first time conversion to Christianity need not have appeared as a risky choice to align oneself with a counter-cultural movement. In a moment the Church went from being an important, but potentially subversive, minority movement to one of the central planks of the state and a potential avenue for official preferment. Not only did Christianity stop being an obstacle to social success or career advancement unless kept covert, adherence to the Church became a positive boon. Not surprisingly, this encouraged an increasing number of individuals to convert. This increase would have been relatively greatest amongst the middle and upper classes who may have previously seen conversion as a threat to their social position. Although a discussion of the precise profile of the Christian community will be left until a later chapter, the fact that all archaeological evidence for Christianity in Britain post-dates the Edict of Milan clearly demonstrates how the sudden alliance of the church and the state led to a large increase in worshippers.

Baptism

The decision to convert was clearly influenced by a range of factors and would certainly have been taken over a period of time. Equally, admission to the Church itself took some time. In today's Church, infants are baptised as an initial introduction to it, and later as a youth or adult will be confirmed as a symbol of their full acceptance into the Church. However, at this period baptism was the central ceremony allowing admittance into the Church. Those wishing to join would be allowed to join the community for most elements of worship, but would be forced to withdraw during the Mass of the Faithful for instruction. This process of initiation and instruction could take up to three years. For many Christians, baptism would not occur until the end of their lives, sometimes not until their deathbed. The obvious implication is that at this period adult baptism would have been common. With the increase in the number of Christians from the early fourth century there were some moves towards infant baptism, but it does not seem to have been the norm.

Although those preparing for baptism were clearly members of the wider Christian community, it was only the sacrament itself that brought them into the heart of the Church. As full members of the Christian community they would be allowed to participate fully in all its ceremonies. The word 'baptism' comes from the Greek for 'to wash'. This emphasises from the very beginning the metaphorical and real importance of washing or immersing to baptism. Although the word was used in the New Testament to describe Jewish ritual washing it soon begun to have a specifically Christian influence.

The importance of some kind of ritual cleansing is widely found in many religions, and it usually emphasised a symbolic washing or ritual as well as physical washing. It was inevitably linked to a wider range of laws about purity and contamination. Such laws about taboo foods and substances were an important part of Judaism, but one of the innovative factors about Jesus' teaching was his rejection of many these regulations. However, the use of ritual washing as an initiation ceremony is less widely known. Although Christians often look to John the Baptist's baptism of Jesus in the River Jordan, he was likely to have been influenced by a Jewish baptismal rite recorded in the Babylonian Talmud.

Although Jesus' baptism took place in a river, the Church soon felt a desire to formalise the baptismal ceremony and provide a suitable context for it. The ritual required that the water be blessed, and thus a dedicated receptacle for this holy water was required, hence fonts were developed. In many cases a separate structure was built to house the font was also built.

Perhaps the best-known font from Britain is the structure found in the north-west corner of the late Roman fort at Richborough (Kent). This was first recognised by P.D.C. Brown who reassessed earlier excavations by

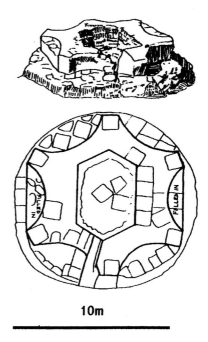

33 *The font from the Roman fort at Richborough.*
May, 1923

10m

Bushe-Fox. It stood just to the north of a probable church (see chapter 3). The small masonry structure was around 2m in diameter (**33**). It had a roughly circular base or foundation built from stone and cobbles. On this sat a hexagonal walled structure with concave sides, giving it a 'cog-like' appearance in plan. Within this was an elongated hexagonal tank. This tank and the hexagonal wall had been covered in a hard pink plaster. On the eastern side, a cut through the wall suggests that a lead drainage pipe had been removed. At some point two of the incurved areas of the hexagonal wall had been filled in. There is no sign of any surrounding structure, though much of the surrounding soil had been removed enmasse by the archaeologists, destroying any potential ephemeral wooden remains.

Another probable font has been found at the Roman religious complex at Ivy Chimneys, Witham (Essex) (**34**). This site was occupied from the Iron Age to the end of the Roman period. In the third century AD a square Romano-British style temple was built; ditches surrounded it. A large pond associated with water channels was probably also built around this time. A new temple was built in the early fourth century. This period of pagan activity was followed by a probable period of Christian activity at the site. The font structure was constructed to the north-east of the pond in a shallow depression. It appeared to have had at least three constructional phases. The initial structure was an octagonal, tile tank. Although it survived to only two

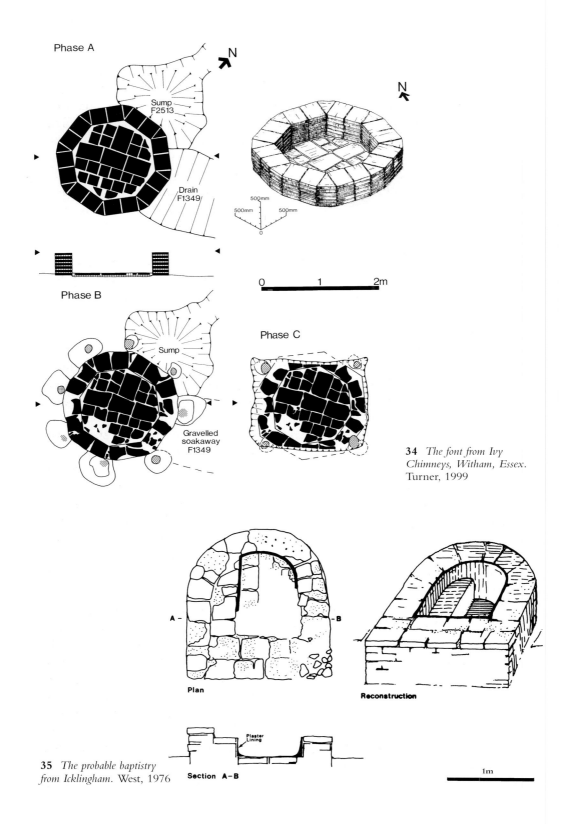

Phase A

Sump
F2513

Drain
F1349

N

Phase B

Sump

Gravelled
soakaway
F1349

Phase C

0   1   2m

500mm

500mm   500mm

0

34 *The font from Ivy Chimneys, Witham, Essex.* Turner, 1999

A ——————— B

Plan

Reconstruction

Plaster Lining

Section A-B

35 *The probable baptistry from Icklingham.* West, 1976

1m

courses it is likely that it was originally higher, and would have been at least 0.4m deep. In the second phase, the tile wall was reduced in height and the wall was replaced by an octagonal timber lining, which was supported by a post-hole at each corner of the tank. At this time a soakaway was probably dug. In its final phase, the depression in which the font sat was partially filled in, which had the effect of placing the font in a pit. At this point, a rectangular wood-lined box replaced the octagonal wooden tank.

The third upstanding cistern-type font was found at the small religious site at Icklingham (Suffolk) (35). To the east of the possible church building was a small masonry structure, known by the excavators as Building C, measuring 1.7m by 1.6m. Like the example from Witham the tank was built from tiles. There was a step in the northern portion of the tank, which was probably partially set into the ground. The inside of the tank was coated with white plaster. There are hints of a possible larger wooden structure surrounding this cistern, as a few traces of wall footings were found, but they were not well-preserved enough to postulate a likely plan.

Another possible font has been found outside the probable church at the Roman fort of Housesteads on Hadrian's Wall. This small cistern stood to the west of the structure. Although this small stone-lined tank has long been recognised, it has not been interpreted as a possible font before. At a later date it was reduced in size, and it has been suggested that this smaller receptacle was used as a grave. However, as we have seen from the examples discussed above it was not uncommon for fonts to go through successive alterations, and it is possible that this later smaller phase was also a font.

As well as these four stone cisterns or tanks there are two other possible baptisteries from Britain with evidence for some kind of masonry substructure. The best known of these comes from the probable church site at Silchester (Hants.). This stands a few metes to the east of the church on the same alignment. There is a rectangular flint platform measuring around 3.3m by 4.3m. In the centre of this foundation is a tile platform (3.2m²). A smaller pit with a flint and tile lining stands between the stone foundation and the church (36).

A similar structure also stood outside the possible church at Butt Road, Colchester (37). Unlike the Silchester structure it was at the west end of the structure, though in this case the apse was at the east. There was a small, square foundation measuring 1.1m by 1.3m. It was built from several courses of tiles. Around this hearth were post-holes indicating that a rectangular wooden structure surrounded it. A number of small pits containing charcoal surrounded the tile structure. The excavators suggested that the central structure was a hearth as there were signs of burning in the middle of it. However, the form of the tile structure and its position relative to the nearby basilica suggest it had the same purpose as the Silchester structure. There is nothing to suggest that the burning was not secondary. Although there was

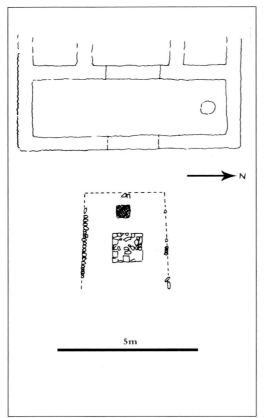

N

5m

36 *Roman font base at Silchester*

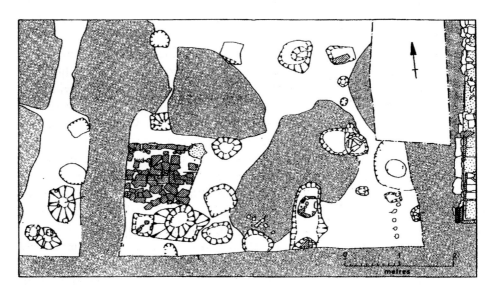

37 *Possible font structure to the west of the church at Butt Road, Colchester.* Crummy *et al.*, 1993

charcoal in the associated pits, charcoal deposits were found across the site and need not have been derived from the burning on the tile structure.

A final group of structures that need to be considered are a number of water features from Roman villas, which may have had a dual purpose. The precise function of this site has been debated. Some have seen it as a luxurious villa, typical of south-western Britain. Others have suggested it may have been a high-status religious site. Certainly a small religious structure stood near the main villa building and another possible religious building stood north-east of the house, though it was destroyed in the nineteenth century and is poorly understood. Built into the hill on the north-west of the house was a further small apsidal building containing an octagonal stone cistern, which was fed by a natural spring (**38**). The water was subsequently piped into the main house. At some point in the fourth century a number of the stone slabs that edged this pool had small *chi-rho* symbols carved into them. However, these slabs were subsequently dismantled and reused elsewhere in the villa. This small building may originally have been a nymphaeum, a small shrine to the spirits of the spring. However, the *chi-rho* symbols suggest that it may have been reused for Christian purposes. Although, as the pool was built before the fourth century, it is unlikely that the number of sides were chosen for its Christian symbolism, this may have encouraged its subsequent reuse. There are other hints of Christian activity at the site: a small metal stamp or seal bearing a *chi-rho* was found in the mid-nineteenth century, though this has now been lost. A small silver spoon bearing the inscription CENSORINE GAUDEAS (Censorine rejoice) was found; the phrase GAUDEAS is known on objects of certain Christian origin from Germany, though it has also been recorded on object of more neutral identity.

Although without overt Christian symbols, a number of other octagonal pools are known from villas in south-west Britain, including Dewlish (Dorset), Lufton (Somerset) and Holcombe (Devon). Dominic Perring has noticed that although situated within bath suites these rooms were not entered through the normal sequence of differently heated rooms, but instead stood apart from the main rooms and had a separate entrance (**39**). He has suggested that these rooms may have been used as baptisteries. Possible Gnostic Christian content has been highlighted by him in some mosaics found in villas in this area, including Hinton St Mary and Frampton. Whilst it is not certain that these structures or the Chedworth pool were built or used permanently as baptisteries the possibility that they had some Christian use, if only occasionally, should not be discounted, especially considering their octagonal shape. They may have formed part of possible proto-monastic estate or house churches, such as were well-known in southern Gaul.

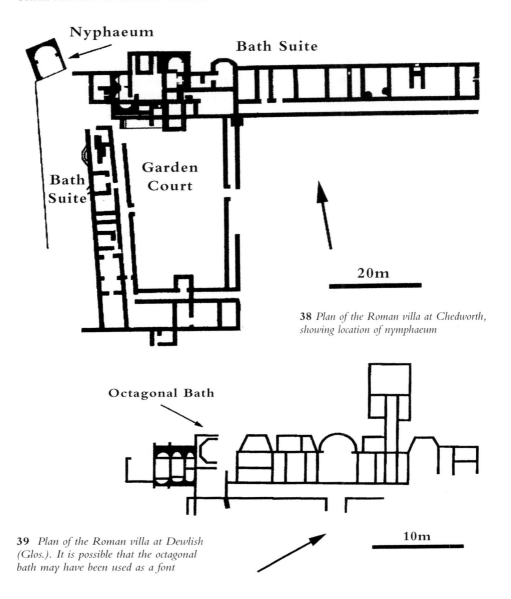

38 *Plan of the Roman villa at Chedworth, showing location of nymphaeum*

39 *Plan of the Roman villa at Dewlish (Glos.). It is possible that the octagonal bath may have been used as a font*

Baptismal lead tanks

Roman Britain is unique in having produced a series of lead tanks bearing Christian symbols. These circular containers are not found elsewhere in the Roman Empire, though over twenty examples have been found in England. Many carry simple decorations, and their exteriors are often divided into panels by vertical banding. They vary slightly in size, the largest being 0.97m in diameter and the smallest 0.46m. It is clear from these motifs that many had some form of Christian function (**40**). A Christian identity is apparent from the range of religious symbols that they have been decorated with. The classic early Christian *chi-rho* symbol has been found on at least eight of these tanks, such those found at Ashton (Northants.) and Pulborough (West Sussex). In one case, on the tanks found at Icklingham (Suffolk) in 1939, the *chi-rho* symbols were flanked by an alpha and omega (**41**). Other such decorations are also known. A recently found tank from Flawborough (Notts.) bore the inscription VTERE EELIX, a slightly misspelt variant of the well-known Late Roman phrase UTERE FELIX meaning something along the lines of 'use well' or 'use with good fortune'. A similar inscription, with an identical spelling mistake was found on the remains of a lead casket from Thorpe (Notts.), suggesting that the two may have been made in the same workshop. On either side of the inscription and just below it lie a total of four simple human figures holding their hands above them in the position known as the *orans* posture, which was typically that used for prayer in the early Christian church (figures in similar poses are known from the painted wall-plaster at Lullingstone).

The most important decorative element on any of these tanks is a small figural frieze shown on a tank found at Walesby (Lincs) (**42**). It consists of three panels, each containing three figures. In the left- and right-hand panels stand three male figures in short cloaks and tunics. In the central panel stands a naked woman flanked by two clothed women. This scene almost certainly depicts a part of the baptismal ceremony, with the naked candidate being lead to the font by helpers. The frieze appears to indicate that the figures are

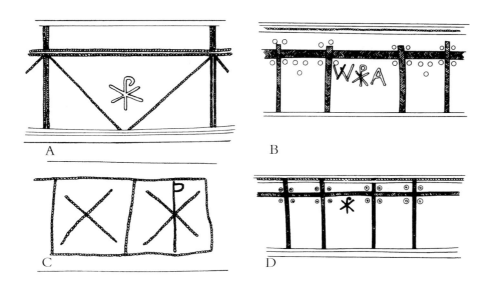

40 *Decoration on Christian lead tanks. A, Ashton, B & D, Icklingham, C, Pulborough*

standing within some kind of structure, though it is unclear whether the architectural elements are meant to represent a baptistery or are merely conventional framing devices for the figures, such as is common in late Roman art. Frustratingly, although baptism is depicted the actual font itself is not shown. This means that although these tanks were certainly involved in the ritual of baptism, their precise function is not known. Although in much of the Roman Empire the central element of the sacrament was the bodily immersion of the candidate in water, Charles Thomas has argued that the baptismal rite in Roman Britain involved *affusion*, the pouring of the holy water over the unclothed individual. He has pointed out that neither the lead tanks nor the masonry fonts were large enough to allow baptism by immersion. However, although baptism by affusion is likely, this does not necessarily mean that these tanks were fonts. It is noticeable that at Icklingham where the remains of at least three of these lead tanks have been found there is also a tile font. It is unlikely that these lead tanks would have been used as fonts, when there was already a permanent purpose-built structure on the site. Multiple lead tanks have also been found at Bourton-on-the-Water (Glos.) and Ashton (Northants). Other possible functions for the fonts need consideration. Dorothy Watts has suggested that they were used for the rite of *pedilavium*, a ritual washing of the feet. This was a

41 *Lead tank from Icklingham (Suffolk).* Copyright British Museum

42 *Reconstruction of the decorative frieze from the lead tank found at Walesby (Lincs.) showing possible baptism.* Thomas, 1981

common part of the baptismal ceremony in much of the Empire, and in the fourth century was carried out by priests rather than bishops after the actual baptism in the font. This rite must be considered as a possibility. However, they may also have had a more general use as containers of holy water. Containers were used to hold holy water for more general ritual washing, as well as for blessing. In some rites the faithful were sprinkled with the holy water on entering the church, and baptismal water was sometimes retained for its curative powers. The precise function of these tanks ultimately remains uncertain, though the scene on the Walesby tank makes it clear that they were involved in some the baptismal rite in some way.

Wells, springs and rivers

As well as using purpose-built baptisteries and fonts, it is quite possible that less obvious features may have been used for baptismal ceremonies. Evidence from the *Life of St Germanus*, which claims to record the activity of the saint in Britain in AD 429 tells of the mass baptism of British troops after a battle with Anglo-Saxons; it implies that they were baptised in a nearby river. In the seventh century Paulinus used rivers to baptise the Northumbrians of Yeavering and Catterick. However, these recorded examples are all of mass baptisms, and there is no clear evidence that such practices ever occurred in Roman Britain. The use of a river for conversion also clearly mirrors Jesus' baptism in the Jordan by John and may have become a literary convention, as much as a record of reality.

However, there is evidence that some wells may have been used for some kind of baptismal purpose. A number of possible Roman churches appear to have incorporated wells or were clearly aligned on wells. Although architecturally elaborated, the possible Christianised nymphaeum at Chedworth was focused over a natural spring. At Witham (Essex), the tile-built font is constructed to the west of a large pond, which was open in the same period, and appears to have become filled up at the same time as the font fell out of use.

In the possible cathedral at Colchester House in London a well was sited in the central aisle of the structure just in front of the chancel. This almost exactly mirrors the position of a well found in the cathedral of St Thecla in Milan. The church at Silchester was also built to the east of a small well, which may also have had been used as a source for water for baptism.

Spatial organisation of baptism

The evidence for the architectural context of baptism from Roman Britain shows a range of spatial arrangements. The probable fonts or font bases from Silchester, Housesteads, Icklingham and Butt Road are all aligned centrally either west or east of the main church structure. This may have been for liturgical reasons, and it is probable that the baptismal rite was integrated into a wider religious service, with an element of ceremonial procession. It is possible in these cases that the church and baptismal area were constructed at the same time, with thought being given to the wider relationship between the two elements. However, in other cases the relationship between the two appears to be less focused. For example, at Richborough the font was located to the north of the apse. This may have been for practical reasons; pressure on space may not have allowed a more linear arrangement. However, this lateral arrangement of baptisteries is very common on the Continent, and it is possible that Richborough, with its proximity to mainland Europe may have copied developments abroad. Although no structure was found surrounding the Richborough font base, the nature of the discovery of the monument may have meant that its remains, particularly if built of wood, were not recognised. The general lack of evidence for the substantial baptisteries found on the continent is not surprising. Although widespread across much of the Roman Empire they are not found in northern Gaul either. In fact only one such structure is known north of the Loire, a six-sided baptistery from Portbail (Manche).

In many cases, particularly where only lead tanks have been found, but also at Witham, there is no convincing evidence for a church at all. It may simply be that the remains of the church have not been found yet. However, there are several examples from the Continent where the baptisteries are not located adjacent to the church. At Tours the main baptistery was sited outside the city away from the main church, whilst at Poitiers the baptistery is over 100m from the cathedral. The unclear relationship between possible baptismal sites is important as it has implications about the pastoral organisation of the ceremony. At this period bishops were the only priests entitled to administer the sacrament, but many of the sites discussed above either have no church or are unlikely to have been the seats of bishops. This means that bishops must have either travelled around their areas carrying out baptisms, rather than the candidates travelling to the cathedral. One implication of this is that the numbers of people being baptised was enough to make it worth the bishop visiting to carry out the ceremony, rather than having centralised ceremonies. This general pattern of non-episcopal baptisteries was found in Gaul in the later fourth century. Monastic sites such as Lérins and small towns such as Civaux (Vienne) all had baptisteries by this time.

The precise pattern of conversion to Christianity in Roman Britain is perhaps ultimately irrecoverable. However, it is likely that conversion followed the same broad stages as set out elsewhere in the Empire. The earliest communities were probably small, and likely to have been limited to London and perhaps one or two of the other major cities. The freedom of the Church led to a rapid increase in its membership, though as we have seen becoming a member of the congregation did not lead immediately to baptism. This only occurred once a strict course of education had been completed. The baptismal rite probably involved affusion, with the holy water being poured over the candidate. There is no evidence for the large, architecturally elaborate baptisteries found on the Continent, though the bases for a number of fonts have been recognised, indicating that the use of some form of permanent structure for the baptismal ceremony was possible. The series of lead tanks bearing Christian imagery, that are unique to Britain, are almost certainly related to the baptismal rite, though their exact function is still debatable. However, whilst baptism may have provided full membership to the Church, with the right to participate fully in the Eucharist, there was more to being a Christian than celebrating these sacraments. Whilst joining together in the Mass may have brought together individual congregations, Christianity would have been visible outside the Church in many ways. It is these external representations of the religions that will be explored in the next chapter.

5

BEING CHRISTIAN

For Christians living in Roman Britain the highlights of their religious life would have been the celebration of the Eucharist and participation in other religious celebrations. However, religion was not limited to high days and holidays. Expressions of religious belief, both pagan and Christian, would have been normal parts of everyday life. Religion would have had an impact on all aspects of day-to-day routine for many people. Most settlements would have had some kind of small shrine or focal point of worship, and mythological and sacred images appeared on all sorts of objects, from simple pots to extravagant mosaics and gold vessels.

The range of explicitly religious symbols used in these early days of Christianity were limited. When the Church was an illegal sect it would have not been deemed wise for it to express its religious beliefs overtly. Indeed, there are no clear examples of Christian art from Britain that can be unequivocally identified as belonging to the third century or earlier. Although in other parts of the Empire, where Christian communities were larger, they may have had a greater sense of self-identity that allowed them to create more overtly religious art. Indeed a number of extremely important pieces of Christian art belong to this period. The elaborate scheme of wall painting from the small house church from Dura Europos (Syria) was destroyed by the Sassanids by the 250s. Equally many of the graves in the catacombs of Rome, the burial place of Christians and others were decorated with distinctly Christian images from the third century. However, in both Rome and Dura Europos the art was displayed in primarily private spaces. Although similar art may have existed in Britain the poor survival of wall paintings and other aspects of architectural decoration has meant that early private religious art of Christian nature is non-existent. These early elements of Christian art from elsewhere in the Empire appear to have had the aim of buttressing the Church's sense of self-worth and providing a distinct identity to a small community under great pressure. It was aimed primarily at other members of the Christian Church rather than the wider community as a whole.

When Constantine opened the arms of the Roman state to Christianity he instantly rearranged the relationship between the two. The Church went from being a barely tolerated and sometimes persecuted sect to the ideological bastion of the Empire. For the first time Christians had the legal legitimacy and economic wherewithal to 'advertise' to society as a whole. As we have seen in the realm of architecture, the Church had to search for new modes of expressing itself and needed to acclimatise itself to this new-found religious freedom. Not surprisingly it is only in the fourth century that a number of distinctly Christian symbols begin to emerge as the Church underwent a period of 'corporate rebranding'. This new range of overt Christian symbols means that from the early fourth century there appears to be a sudden increase in the level of Christianity in Britain. Obviously this was partly due to the absolute increase in the number of Christians, but also those who were already believers began to develop the artistic vocabulary they needed to express themselves.

The consequence of this chance to experiment and develop artistically was the appearance of a number of distinctive symbols or signs that came to represent Christianity. At this early stage a number of images, which we now associate with the Church, had not yet appeared. The simple cross, either with equal arms or a longer stem did not start to be used by Christians until the late fourth century, and even then only amongst communities around the Mediterranean Rim. The crucifix, showing Jesus crucified upon the cross did not develop until even later. The earliest and most widespread symbol was the so-called *chi-rho*. This first appeared as a capital letter P overlaid with a capital X. These were, in fact, the Greek letters *chi* and *rho*. These stood for the first two letters of the Greek word *Christos*, meaning 'anointed one'. Although examples are known from before 313 it was quickly associated with the cross image seen by Constantine on the eve of the Battle of the Milvian Bridge. This version of the *chi-rho* is usually known as the 'Constantinian' *chi-rho* to distinguish it from a later version (**43a**). The later version appeared as the letter P with a simple stroke across its downward shaft, sometimes known as the *rho* cross or later *chi-rho* (**43b**). This began to appear from the later fourth century. Both types of *chi-rho* were commonly associated with the Greek letters *alpha* (A, ℈) and omega (W, ω). These were the first and last letters of the Greek alphabet and referred to a passage from the Revelations: 'I am Alpha and Omega says the Lord God, which is and which was and which is to come' (*Rev.* 1.8, see also *Rev.* 21.6). They often appeared as the Latin letters A and W. These could be seen in a range of contexts, including the handle of a strainer from the Water Newton treasure, the painted wall-plaster from Lullingstone and the pewter bowl found near Ely (Cambs.) (**44**). Its precise meaning, if not its more general significance may not always have been understood, as number of objects such as a lead tank from Icklingham and votive object from Water Newton show the letters upside-down or back to front (**45**). There were a number of variants of the *chi-rho*, both with and without the A and Ω symbols. They might be shown enclosed within a circle, perhaps

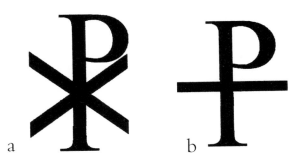

43 (a) Constantinian chi-rho
(b) rho cross

a   b

echoing the celebratory wreath known as the *corona*. In other cases the loop of
the P either did not completely meet the vertical shaft or there was a slight
hook, making the P appear more like an R. This appears to be a Latinisation
of the Greek *Rho*, and may have indicated the phrases *Christus Rex*. This
appears on several objects from the Water Newton treasure (**46**).

A number of other similar symbols also appear to have developed in this
period. The *iota chi*, a combination of the Greek initials of *Iesous Christos*,
appeared as an X superimposed upon a vertical line. This symbol appeared as
a simple asterisk-like sign. The simple saltire or St Andrew's cross has also been
suggested as being a Christian symbol as has the letter Y, which may have
indicated both the position of Jesus on the cross and the shape of someone
worshipping in the *orans* positions (see below). However, these symbols were
also common decorative motifs used on a wide range of clearly non-Christian
objects. Even when symbols such as the saltire appear on probable Christian
objects such as the lead tanks from Bourton-on-the-Water (Glos.) it is not clear
whether they carry a religious meaning or are merely common design
elements used as decoration. It is probable that Christian writers and apologists
often imputed a religious meaning onto pre-existing symbols in an attempt to
imbue all aspects of life with a wider sense of meaning. However, it is
dangerous to suggest a Christian identification to an object on the basis of these
simple symbols alone.

The fourth century also saw the development of ways of representing individuals as Christians. This can clearly be seen in the depiction of individuals in
the *orans* position. This described the praying position commonly used in the
late Roman church. The worshipper stood with hands raised up at shoulder
level, a position still used by modern priests while celebrating mass. Figures in
this position are shown on the wall paintings from Lullingstone and on a
recently discovered lead tank from Flawborough (Notts.). Other images of
Christian worship come from the image of a probable baptism on the lead tank
from Walesby (Lincs.) (the two figures are also shown on an unusual lead casket
from East Stoke (Somerset)). Only the upper half of this object survives. It is

44 Chi-rhos *with alpha and omega. (left) from wall painting at Lullingstone; (centre) pewter bowl from the Isle of Ely; (right) from Water Newton treasure*

45 *Examples of upside down or reversed alpha and omega (left) from Water Newton hoard (right) from lead tank found at Icklingham*

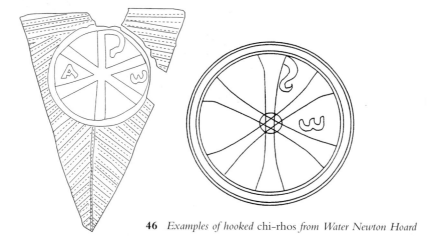

46 *Examples of hooked* chi-rhos *from Water Newton Hoard*

decorated with a *chi-rho* and the inscription *utere felix* ('use happily'). The inscription is flanked by these two small figures that wear long robes. It is not clear precisely who they are meant to be, though they are most likely to represent Christian worshippers.

Other conventions widely used in the medieval period, such as the halo around the head, had not yet achieved a purely Christian meaning. More properly known as a nimbus (Latin for cloud) it was widely used in classical Roman and Greek art to indicate that a figure was a god or a hero. It was slow to enter Christian art. It first appeared around the head of Jesus in the fourth century, but in these contexts it was usually decorated with a *chi-rho*. By the fifth century it was also used for angels and prophets, and by the sixth century square nimbuses were used to indicate a living person of holiness. Thus, the nimbused figure depicted on a fourth-century wall painting from Malton (East Yorks.) is unlikely to have been a Christian (**47**).

Christianity and the state

It is, however, not enough to merely identify examples of Christian symbols, we need to explore the way in which they were used. The decision to deploy a Christian image may have been governed by many factors. It is not safe to assume that just because an object appeared with a religious symbol it was either made or used by a Christian. This problem is most complex with the *chi-rho*. This symbol had a double-life in the fourth century. Although it is

47 *The head of a female figure with nimbus from Malton (N. Yorks.).* Smith, 2000

commonly believed that its appearance at the Battle of the Milvian Bridge led to its widespread use by the Christian community, it also indelibly linked it with the imperial House of Constantine and indeed the position of emperor in general. The tension in the meaning of this sign paralleled the wider tension between the Church and state in the fourth century. Whilst loyalty to one implied a loyalty to the other, the relationship could often be complicated and difficult. Emperors tried to intervene in Church affairs, for example Constantine's early involvements in Church councils and Maximus' persecution of Priscillanism in Spain. Equally, powerful bishops, such as Ambrose of Milan increasingly attempted to exercise influence on secular affairs within the Empire, and were on occasions able to force emperors into humiliating reversals of policy.

The use of the *chi-rho* on many objects in Britain may tell us as much about the use of imperial imagery as religious symbolism. The clearest examples of the *chi-rho* being deployed in such an imperial context comes in its appearance on coinage issued by Magnentius. Bronze *nummi* minted in Amiens have a large *chi-rho* flanked by an A and Ω on the obverse side (**48**).

Another example of the use of the *chi-rho* in official contexts comes from a series of tin or pewter ingots from London (**49**). These were all recovered from the Thames during dredging works; several were found near Battersea and others nearer Wandsworth. Eight had the name Syagrius and a Constantinian *chi-rho* encircled by the phrase SPES IN DEO ('hope in God') cast on them, the other two carried the name Suagrius (presumably a variant on Syagrius) and a stamp bearing a chi-rho flanked by an A and Ω. The name

48 *Bronze nummus bearing a* chi-rho *symbol. It was minted in Amiens in the mid-fourth century AD.* Copyright British Museum

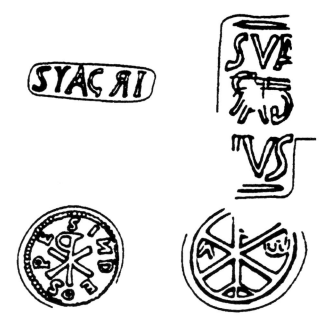

49 *Stamps from pewter ingots in the River Thames in London* After Mawer, 1995

Syagrius has been identified as referring to the Syagrius who was a late Roman ruler in Gaul; based in Soissons, he was defeated by the Franks in the late fifth century. However, the style of *chi-rho* suggests an earlier date, and there is no reason to assume anything later than a fourth-century date. Instead he is more likely to be the official responsible for the production and export of the metal. The *chi-rho* is almost certainly an official stamp indicating imperial control of metal production. This probability is also reflected in the presence of a *chi-rho* on silver ingots that formed part of a hoard of fourth-century Roman precious metal objects found in Balline (Co. Limerick). Similar *chi-rho* symbols have been found on metal ingots from elsewhere in the Empire. However, one other possibility that should not be discounted is that the Church may have controlled metal production. The possible control of the economic production by the Church may also be indicated by the salt-pan from Shavington (Cheshire), which appears to carry the name of a bishop. It is possible that the church had been granted control over elements of mineral extraction in Britain.

It is possible that the *chi-rho* symbols from a series of seals and seal rings may also have an official function. A lead seal with a *chi-rho* cross was found in the forum at Silchester. It was flanked by a three letters, probably P, C and M. These have been identified as standing for P(ROVINCIA) M(AXIMA) C(AESARIENSIS), the Roman province in which Silchester was situated (**50**). This suggests a clear administrative function. In other cases the situation is not so clear-cut. A gold seal ring has been found at Brentwood (Essex). A

50 *Lead seal bearing* chi-rho *symbol from Silchester, 1:1.* Mawer, 1995

circular wreath surrounds the simple Constantinian *chi-rho* (**51**). Another gold ring from an unidentified site in Suffolk has the image of a bird pecking at a tree or bush, standing above a *rho* cross. The cross appeared in reverse, but would have appeared the correct way round if it had been used to imprint a wax seal. Two silver rings bearing *chi-rhos* one Constantinian and the other a *rho* cross, were found at the Roman villa of Fifehead Neville (Dorset). Other similar rings include a silver one from Thruxton (Hants.), a bronze one from Richborough (Kent) and a jet example from Bagshot (Surrey). All of these rings, except possibly the latter, are likely to have been seal rings. However, who did they belong to? They could have belonged to Imperial or local government officials, private individuals or Christian dignitaries. The lack of distinct personal indicators may imply that they are less likely to have been private seals, suggesting a religious or secular provenance. However, from the evidence it is impossible to distinguish between the two. This is the crux of the problem; the imagery and symbolism used by church officials and administrators was drawn from the same repertoire of sources. In some cases the same person may have had dual roles. We know from the *Life of St Patrick* that his father had been both a deacon and a decurion. The two classes of official are likely to have been recruited from the same social groups. It is not always possible to draw a sharp line between the two. Bishops certainly increasingly had both secular and religious roles.

The relationship between the state and religion is also highlighted by a series of belt fittings, buckles and strap-ends found in Britain. They were manufactured in a style that was once thought to be Germanic. However, they can now be seen as part of a widely distributed class of late Roman belt buckles. Belt sets were of great symbolic importance in the late Roman world. Indicators of status and marks of authority, they are thought to have been worn mainly by members of the *comitatenses*, the late Roman field army, though members of the imperial civil administration may also have used them. Interestingly, these belt sets appear to have been manufactured locally in Britain, and there are such close similarities between some examples they probably came from the same workshop. Apart from a belt hook from Sandy (Bucks.) (**52**) these artefacts did not carry *chi-rhos*; in fact a large number bore no kind of religious

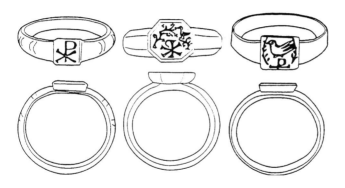

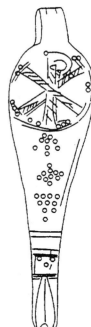

51 *Rings with* chi-rho *symbols. (left) Fifehead Neville, Dorset; (centre) unknown site in Suffolk; (right) Fifehead Neville, Dorset 2:1.* Mawer, 1995

52 (Right) *Bronze strap-end from Sandy (Beds.) decorated with an incised chi-rho. Drawn by Mike Bishop in* Mawer, 1995

53 (Below) *Belt-buckles carrying peacock imagery; (top) Penycorddyn, Clwyd; (middle)* Tripontium, *Warks.; (bottom) Stanwick, North Yorks. Drawn by Mike Bishop in* Mawer, 1995

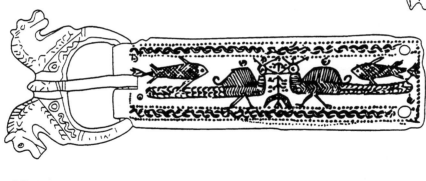

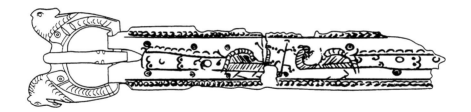

symbolism. However, a number of them had images of peacocks (**53**). Whilst the peacock is not thought of as a symbol of Christianity today, it had a religious resonance in the fourth century. The flesh of the peacock was traditionally believed to be incorruptible, and for St Augustine it became a symbol of immortality: 'For who but God the Creator of all things has given to the flesh of the peacock its antiseptic property?' (*De Civ Dei* 21:4). This may explain its frequent appearance on early Christian tombstones. It only appears on two other Christian objects from Britain, a pewter bowl from the Isle of Ely and a second bowl of unknown provenance. However, it is most widely found on these belt sets. Unusually, despite its widespread use in such contexts in Britain only one has been found on the Continent, and even this example, from Westerwanna in Germany, was probably of British manufacture. The peacock appears in two locations on the British belts — either on the buckle plate, where there are usually two birds opposing each other, or on strap-ends when either a single peacock or a peacock and a griffin are shown.

The presence of a discrete set of official dress items carrying Christian symbols is significant; especially as similar belt sets from elsewhere do not carry this imagery. The distribution of these objects is mainly confined to the civilian zone of Britain, with a notable outlier at Penycorddyn (Clwyd) (**54**). This

54 *Map of belt sets with Christian imagery in Britain*

pattern is compatible with both the presumed distribution of the *comitatenses* and the imperial civil service. The fact that such belts were produced locally within Britain means that the choice of imagery on them was likely to have been determined by those commissioning their manufacture. Unlike elsewhere in Europe, whoever was responsible for this choice was clearly concerned that they had a clearly Christian identity. However, they used an image which although widespread on the Continent was uncommon in Britain. Does this suggest unfamiliarity with the nature of Romano-British Christianity by the person who ordered their manufacture? Until there is a clearer understanding of the organisation of their production and distribution we cannot say more.

Two other parts of possible official regalia with Christian symbols have been found. A large silver buckle decorated with geometrical patterns was found amongst a hoard of over 150 silver objects discovered in the hillfort of Traprain Law (E. Lothian). An A and Ω appeared on the plate of the buckle with an outline of dots. Two silver chip-carved strap-ends were also found with this buckle, and they were probably part of an official belt set. These are one of the most elaborate belt sets known from Britain. Belts were not the only objects which had official connotations. A class of brooches, known as crossbow brooches after their shape, were widely used across the Roman Empire as a mark of status. An unusual variant of a crossbow brooch from Sussex was decorated with a *rho* cross of punched dots (**55**). Although this is the only example of such a brooch with Christian symbolism from Britain, they are more widely spread on the Continent. Good examples include an elaborate brooch from Basel, which was decorated with a *chi-rho* and a portrait of the emperor.

The combined evidence of seal rings, ingots, coinage and belt sets shows that in the late Roman period the state was interested in projecting a Christian image, closely binding the Church and Empire together. However, in each case the context of the production and intended use of the objects is different. Coins were intended for mass circulation, and were usually minted outside Britain. The use of coinage was quite extensive by this time, and the clear religious imagery on the coins would have been widespread. Whilst it would have functioned to indicate the Emperor in Rome, Milan or Trier was Christian coins would not have indicated the religious allegiance of those whom they came in contact with. Coins with overt Christian imagery were in a minority, most issue carrying more secular imagery.

Seals, seal rings and the marks on ingots, however, were clearly intended to identify an individual, either personally or *ex officio*, and hence the expression of a Christian identity was more precise. People who came in contact with these seals would understand that the person who had stamped them identified themselves, if only officially, as a Christian. However, the contexts in which seals were used would have been limited. Although, as the ingots suggest, some commercial products could bear a seal-like imprint, in most cases

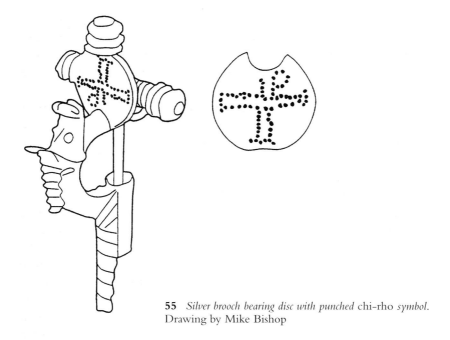

55 *Silver brooch bearing disc with punched* chi-rho *symbol.*
Drawing by Mike Bishop

the seals would have secured official or important documents. These would have passed through the hands of a relatively small group of probably high-status and literate individuals.

However, the belt sets when worn would have been quite visible. As civil servants and soldiers would have worn them it is likely that they were seen by large sections of the populace. We know from visual representations that military shields were often decorated with the *chi-rho* symbol. This appearance of obvious Christian symbols on objects carried or worn by the representatives of the Roman state would have sent a powerful signal. As far as the state was concerned the absolute number of Christians was not important; the crucial thing was that the administrative and military wings of government were clearly identified as being allied with the Church.

Christian art and domestic space

So far, this chapter has focused upon the representations of Christianity on objects and artefacts, but these were not the only places where such art appeared. As our earlier discussion of churches hinted at, architectural space could often be elaborately decorated, utilising both wall paintings and mosaic floors.

The evidence for Christian wall painting is limited. We have already seen the best example, the fortuitously preserved painted schemes from the house church at Lullingstone. These include *chi-rho* symbols and figures praying in the

Christian *orans* position. Another possible group of Christian wall paintings survive in fragments from inside the mausolea structures at the Poundbury cemetery outside Dorchester (Dorset). The fragments of painted wall–plaster were recovered from the inside of mausoleum R8. The variable preservation of the plaster means it is not possible to fully reconstruct the scenes depicted, but Christopher Sparey-Green has isolated several elements. A number of figures, both male and female appear to be shown. They seem to be carrying staffs or rods, which are probably markers of status. The figures show great variation, and the difference in their sizes may have been intended to depict some kind of relative hierarchy amongst the group. At least three of the figures seem to be wearing purple robes, perhaps indicating high status. Importantly for our purposes, fragments of a *chi-rho* symbol have been identified to the right of one of the figures. Whilst it is possible that this was a depiction of a Biblical scene it is more likely that they were representations of the family who had used the mausoleum. The rods bring to mind a fragment of painted wall plaster from Malton (East Yorks.). In this latter example the rods have a cross–shaped terminal, though this is unlikely to be of religious significance. Other elements of the Poundbury painting seem to include fragments of a possible semi–aerial view of a group of buildings, possibly a town. Similar views are known in a Christian context from a mosaic at St Maria Maggiore in Rome. The plaster from mausoleum R9 was much more poorly preserved but appeared to also show a figural group. Whatever the precise interpretation of these scenes is the present of a *chi-rho* makes it clear that the family were determined to represent their religious identity in their tomb.

There are also a number of mosaics with certain Christian imagery, as well as a number of more ambiguous examples. The best-known Christian mosaic comes from the Roman villa of Hinton St Mary (Dorset). It was found in a large rectangular room divided into two unequal sections. In the central roundel of the mosaic in the larger room were the head and shoulders of a youth. Behind his head was a large Constantinian *chi-rho*. It is hard to see this individual as anyone except Jesus. Although there are similarities between the figure and that of imperial portraiture, he is not an emperor; he wears the tunic and *pallium* (cloak) typical of other early depictions of Christ.

The *chi-rho* also appears on another mosaic, Frampton (Dorset). It also is found within a suite of two conjoined rooms. The *chi-rho* appears in the western of two rooms just on the edge of an apse. The precise date of these mosaics is uncertain, but they are both likely to have been made in the early to mid–fourth century, perhaps the 340s. The similarity in the workmanship between the two and their close proximity has also suggested to some that they were produced by the same group of mosaic artists. They are also similar in subtler, but equally important ways; they all have a similar location within the house. The suites of rooms in which they were sited were the main reception rooms of the villa buildings. It was in these audience chambers that the villa owner would have received visitors, including neighbours, relatives and clients. In both cases they have a central position in the mosaic scheme. The apse at Frampton would have been where the villa owner sat, and the *chi-rho* would have been immediately in front of him facing outwards. The *chi-rho* and the villa owner were clearly visually juxtaposed.

However, despite the overt Christian symbolism in these mosaics, the religious imagery on them is complex. The other motifs on the Hinton St Mary pavement include scenes of hounds hunting deer. On the contiguous mosaic in the next room there are further hunting scenes flanking an image from the Classical myth of Bellerophon killing the monster, Chimaera. At Frampton the main mosaic depicts the same scene, as well as four pairs of lovers – the mosaic in the next room shows images of Dionysius riding on a leopard. Flanking a depiction of a bearded head, directly opposite the *chi-rho* was a mosaic inscription reading 'NEPTUNI VERTEX REG[I]MEN SORTITI MOBILE VENTIS SCUL[P]TUM CUI CERULEA [EST] DELFINIS CINCTA DUOB[US], which translates as 'The head of Neptune to whose lot fell the kingdom of the sea scoured by the winds is figured here, his deep-blue brow girt by a pair of dolphins'. This combination of pagan and Christian imagery appears curious. A similar combination comes from Lullingstone (Kent). Despite the presence of the Christian wall paintings in the building, the mosaic in the main reception room showed scenes of Europa and the Bull and Bellerophon and the Chimaera. The presence of Christian objects from sites with Classical mosaics provide more examples of this combination of paganism and Christianity. Fish and sea-monsters are shown on a mosaic from Fifehead Neville (Dorset), which has also produced two *chi-rho* rings, and Bacchic imagery appeared on a mosaic at Thruxton (Hants.), a site which produce another silver *chi-rho* ring.

The meaning of this combination of motifs has long been debated. The classical imagery may be taken at face value and seen as a reflection of a lightly held paganism or the absorption of classical elements into Christianity. However, it is possible to understand these schemes in more depth. Although today we strongly contrast the scenes of pagan religious scenes with Christian images, this distinction need not have been made at the time. In the fourth century the literary education of the elite, both pagan and Christian, was still rooted within the classical canon. Even bishops were meant to know their Horace and Virgil. This knowledge, known as *paideia*, also included knowledge of rhetoric, grammar and oratory. This highly complex and intellectual outlook was deliberately cultivated and may have provided a unifying sense of identity, which helped to bring together the elites of the Roman Empire. This kind of cultural knowledge would have been essential for progress within the imperial administration.

The best way in which this knowledge could be expressed was through a refined expression of good taste in the art and architecture. This would have encouraged the commissioning of mosaics depicting mythological scenes, as well as sculptures and wall paintings. These would have acted not just as works of art to be viewed, but also as foci for discussion and springboards into a consideration of the more arcane aspects of *paideia*. An underlying trend in the contemporary thought of the time was the emphasis on classical myths as allegory. They were not meant to be understood literally, but as referring to a higher meaning. This meant that the depiction of pagan mythology could refer to a range of theological and spiritual themes, beyond those which they depicted. It was this potential for referring to something beyond that made these images so flexible and allowed them to sit so comfortably with orthodox Christian imagery. Such a reading of these images serves to underline the audience for whom these mosaics were intended. They were aimed at the members of the villa owners' circle who had the sophistication and cultural *savoir-faire*, which would allow them to understand the allusions, contained within them. For those without the necessary social knowledge to interpret the rich allegorical messages within the mosaics, the central position of the *chi-rho* at Frampton and the head of Jesus at Hinton St Mary reassured the view of the underlying religious identity of the villa owner.

However, the matter is more complex than this. As we have seen, the choice of classical scenes overtly juxtaposed with Christian images was relatively limited, with Bellerophon and Chimaera occurring in all three cases, and sea imagery appearing at Fifehead Neville and Frampton. The imagery of wild animals and the depiction of Dionysius on a leopard at Frampton suggests an interest in myths associated with both Orpheus and Bacchus.

This suggests that the choice of scene had some meaning to Christians, and they were not chosen as arbitrary indicators of *paideia*. Orpheus has had a long link with Christianity, and was shown in clearly Christian contexts elsewhere. For example Orpheus charming the beasts is shown in the Catacombs of St Priscilla in Rome. Early Church writers, such as Origen, also drew overt comparisons with Jesus and Orpheus, comparing the song of Orpheus with the teachings of Jesus, taming the passions of man and beast. Dominic Perring has also suggested that there was a strong Gnostic element to the Christianity of Romano-British villa owners. Gnostic religious thought, which was found in both paganism and Christianity, had several important elements, including an emphasis on the duality of good and evil that was related to the spiritual and the material. There was an emphasis on the importance of discovering secrets by revelation that would allow the human spirit or soul to escape its physical prison in the body. Images of Bacchus and Dionysius were closely connected with pagan Gnosticism, and the image of Bellerophon and Chimaera had symbolic meanings related to the victory of the spiritual world over the material world. The figure of Neptune at Frampton and the marine imagery from Frampton and Fifehead Neville also found resonances in Gnostic thought linked with the image of the journey of the soul to heaven. The material world was often depicted in Gnosticism as an ocean.

As well as these Gnostic elements associated with evidence for Christianity, many of these themes were widely found in context where there was no sign of the religion. Depictions of Orpheus were not uncommon on mosaics, particularly in the area around Cirencester, as were Bacchus and other elements of Dionysian imagery. If Christianity was influenced by Gnosticism in Britain it had clearly developed in a wider context of Gnostic thought. It is difficult to be certain how far this Gnostic element was a serious element of religious thought, and how far it was merely a significant, but not necessarily profound, element of the prevailing culture of *paideia*.

Hoards and treasure

This combination of pagan imagery and Christian symbolism did not only appear on mosaics. Britain has produced a series of hoards of precious metal objects which mirrored this practice. In 1942 a hoard of 34 silver items was found during ploughing at Mildenhall (Suffolk). This assemblage included eight spoons, of which three were decorated with the *chi-rho* motif (**56**). However, amongst the most important objects from the hoard was the so-called 'Great Dish'. This was decorated with engravings of mythological scenes featuring Bacchus whilst in the centre the head of Oceanus or Neptune was depicted. Further Bacchic scenes appeared on two silver plates from the same hoard. This choice of imagery is almost exactly the same as that appearing on the Frampton mosaic.

The hunting imagery from Hinton St Mary is reflected on the Risley Park Lanx. The original of this dish is now lost, but a faithful copy survives. This shows a boar hunt, whilst around the rim shepherd and other hunting scenes are displayed. The choice of imagery would suggest a pagan identity if it was not for the inscription recording that it had been a gift from Bishop Exuperius. A similar rectangular dish was found in the River Tyne near Corbridge. This showed the god Apollo standing by a shrine accompanied by the goddesses Artemis and Minerva. Again this would not have been connected with Christianity if it had not been for the appearance of the *chi-rho* on other vessels from this group.

Not all of these precious metal hoards contained objects with classical imagery. The most important example is the Water Newton hoard. This large hoard of 27 silver objects and a gold disc was found in 1975 on the site of the small Roman town of *Durobrivae*. This included 16 votive plaques (**57**) and a number of cups, jugs, dishes and flasks. Two silver cups bore inscriptions. One read: INNOCENTIA ET VIVENTIA … RUNT which has been translated as 'Innocentia and Viventia. Dedicated?/offered?' (**58**). Next to this phrase was a *chi-rho* flanked by a A and Ω; the other inscribed cup bore the text: SANCTUM ALTARE TUUM DOMINE SUBNIXUS

56 *Silver spoons from a fourth-century AD hoard found in Mildenhall (Suffolk).*
Copyright British Museum

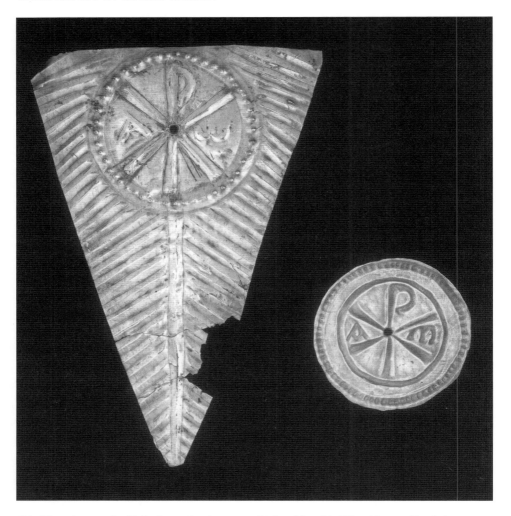

57 *Silver plaque and gold disc from a fourth-century AD hoard found in Water Newton (Cambs.)*
Copyright British Museum

HONORO. This phrase has been roughly translated as 'I humbly honour your altar, O Lord'. Interestingly, the use of the term SANCTUM ALTARE TUUM finds strong echoes in early liturgical texts, and may have been a quote from the order of service for celebrating the Eucharist used by the Romano-British Church. This cup was also decorated with a *chi-rho* flanked by A and Ω. Other objects from this hoard included a flat-based ditch inscribed with the same symbols.

This group of objects was probably deposited in the second half of the fourth century. Its purpose has been debated, but it appears that it was almost certainly a set of liturgical plate used by a local church. This has been established by comparison with other known sets of church plate from elsewhere in the

Empire. As well as showing its similarity to these foreign hoards it is clear that the Water Newton hoard was an exceptionally early example.

The more precise function of many of these items is not entirely clear. The cups may have been chalices used to hold the Communion wine, while the dish may have been a paten, the dish on which the host used by the priest was placed. The flask-shaped containers probably held the water and the wine used in the Eucharist. A strainer, decorated with a *chi-rho* may also have had a liturgical function. Such strainers were frequently used in many contexts in the Roman world, both secular and religious. A fine example of a strainer or an infuser with a silver case was found in the Wallbrook Mithraeum in London. However, strainers also had a clear Christian ritual function, and were used when mixing the water and the wine and removing the bread from the liquid. When decorated with Christian symbols, such as those from Traprain Law and Water Newton, they were probably used in such a way. Another multi-purpose object with occasional religious use are so-called 'picks'. Many suggestions have been made for the function of these metal tools, with a comma-shaped implement at one end. Suggested functions include ear-scoops, nail-cleaners, scoops for applying make-up or even picks for eating snails. However, one such pick, from Canterbury, was decorated with a *chi-rho* (**59**). It may have been a secular object, though owned by a Christian. Alternatively, it may have had the religious function outlined above.

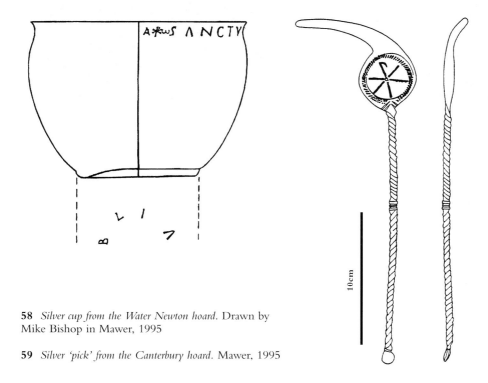

58 *Silver cup from the Water Newton hoard.* Drawn by Mike Bishop in Mawer, 1995

59 *Silver 'pick' from the Canterbury hoard.* Mawer, 1995

A number of other hoards contained objects which may have had liturgical functions. The Traprain Law hoard, although probably brought together as booty from raids or assembled as a tribute to southern Scottish clients of the Roman Empire, contained many intriguing items. As well as the belt fittings discussed above there were many fragments of silver vessels. Pagan classical imagery appeared on many objects, but two silver flasks had Christian images on them. One showed biblical scenes and the other had a *chi-rho* on it. A strainer decorated with a *chi-rho* and the phrase IESUS CHRISTUS was also found in the hoard (**60**).

Another interesting hoard consisted of a number of objects found in the River Tyne between Corbridge and Bywell. As well as the Corbridge Lanx this included a silver flask with the inscription DESIDERI VIVAS ('long live to Desiderius'), which may have been a Christian acclamation. A round-bottomed flat bowl carrying six *chi-rho* symbols was also found; this could have been a chalice.

A further common element of these hoards is a large number of spoons. Roman spoons are usually of two types: those with long handles and those with shorter handles. They are often decorated with the *chi-rho* or carry short inscriptions, such as AUGUSTINE VIVAS ('Augustinus, long life to you') found on a spoon from Dorchester (Dorset). Many possible functions have been suggested for these objects, particularly relating to the administering or mixing of Communion wine. However, these objects are found widely across Britain and are far more common than any other possible liturgical objects. In some cases, even when found with other objects they are the only overtly Christian one. A group of silver objects found in Canterbury in 1962 included four silver ingots, twelve spoons, a necklace and other jewellery and a strainer. Two of the spoons were decorated with a *chi-rho*. The massive Hoxne hoard, deposited in the early fifth century, also contained a Christian component, a group of ten spoons decorated with the *chi-rho* symbol.

The common appearance of names on these objects may suggest that they were small gifts, possibly made on baptism. However, the appearance of spoons in hoards was not simply a Christian practice, and they appear in the Thetford hoard, which contained jewellery, strainers and silver spoons. Many of these spoons bore the name of the god Faunus or names that were related to his cult.

Biblical imagery

So far the discussion of the relationship between Christian and pagan imagery has tended to portray Christian art as primarily symbolic, limited to a small repertoire of religious symbols, whereas pagan art appears to frequently show figurative scenes depicting moments from classical mythology. However, there

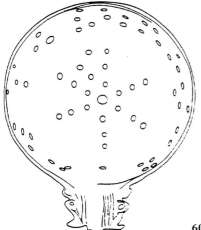

60 *Strainer from Trapian Law.* Curle, 1923

61 *Frieze of biblical scenes from copper plaque on a bucket from Long Wittenham*

are a small number of examples of Christian art showing similar narrative scenes. These all seem to have decorated small metal vessels or containers.

Although long thought to be of early medieval date, a small cup from the Anglo-Saxon cemetery at Long Wittenham (Oxon) is probably of Romano-British origin. It is decorated with a thin sheet of bronze in which a series of decorations have been added in repoussée (**61**). One side of the cup shows a *chi-rho* flanked by A and Ω. On the opposite side of the cup there are three biblical scenes. The central one shows the baptism of Jesus with the name of St John (IOHANNES) appearing above it. To the left is a portrayal of the wedding of Cana, whilst on the right the tax collector Zacchaeus is shown standing in a tree. Martin Henig has pointed out that all three of these scenes show the salvationary power of faith, and has suggested that the object may have been used as a chalice.

Another example of biblical scenes on bronze repoussée work comes from the pagan temple at Uley (**62**). Unlike the Long Wittenham example, the bronze sheet was not attached to another object and had been folded and left as a votive offering. It was probably originally attached to a small box or possibly a cup and showed four biblical scenes: Jesus and the Centurion's servant, Jesus curing a blind man, Jonah sleeping beneath a bush and the sacrifice of Isaac.

Biblical scenes also appeared on a silver flask, which was part of the Traprain Law hoard (**63**). Three of the scenes shown are easy to recognise: Adam, Eve and the serpent, the Adoration of the Magi before a seated Virgin and child, and Moses bringing water from a rock. The fourth scene is partially damaged and harder to interpret; suggestions include the Betrayal, the Arrest of Peter and the Miracle of Quails in the Desert.

Depositing religious objects

As well as exploring the imagery on religious art of this period it is also necessary to consider the context in which it was placed. In the cases of wall paintings and mosaics they have remained in the same location as they were used. However, for smaller objects it is clear that they had complex lives and were found in different contexts to those in which they were used. By considering the 'biography' of these artefacts it is possible to understand a little more about the way in which Roman Christianity used its religious objects.

It is useful to consider the case of the lead tanks or fonts explored earlier in chapter 4. Some tanks have been found in buildings, such as those from Bourton-on-the-Water and some have unrecorded contexts as they were metal-detector finds (for example Brough, Notts.) or were found by ploughing (Walesby, Lincs.). However, a significant number have been found in 'watery' locations. The examples from Ashton (Northants.) were found in a well as was that from Caversham (Berks.). The tank found at Heathrow was located near the top of waterhole which was located in an area that had a long tradition of ritual deposition in such contexts from the late Bronze Age. Others had a riverine context: the Oxborough tank was found by the River Wissey, the Pulborough tank, near the River Arun, the Huntingdon tank from the River Ouse and the Willingham tank from the Fens.

The tradition of using pits or watery places as a location for making ritual deposits has a long history in Europe. In the Iron Age a range of high quality metal objects including swords and shields were often placed in rivers. Over 28 swords, 40 spears, three shields and a helmet have been found in the River Thames alone. All sorts of objects from animal bones to pots also appear to

62 *Piece of copper alloy sheeting showing biblical scenes.* Woodward 1993

have been carefully placed in specially constructed pits. For example, at the Roman temple of Uley offerings included eight nearly complete vessels, tools, weapons and part of a cow were placed in a ritual pit in the first century.

It is clear that whatever their main purpose, the deposition of the fonts is part of a wider phenomenon of ritual deposition in late Roman Britain. These lead tanks are not the only type of late Roman lead or pewter vessels to be found in such ritual contexts. The hoarding and deposition of pewter vessels and tableware is widespread. The vessels themselves mostly date from after *c*.AD 250. Although some writers have argued for a practical reason for their deposition, such as hiding them in times of crisis, the wider consensus is that they were buried for religious reasons. Many of these hoards were found in very similar locations to those in which the Christian lead tanks were found. Pewter plates have been found in rivers at Shepperton (Middlesex) and Verulamium (Herts.), whilst similar hoards have been found in pits or wells at several sites, such as at Stanwick (Northants) and Brislington (Avon). In a more clearly religious context, a wide range of pewter pieces were found in the spring at the centre of the temple complex at Bath. Some of these carried inscriptions dedicating them to the gods.

It might be argued that the deposition of such pewter hoards was essentially a pagan practice, and that Christians would not follow such a rite. The

63 *Biblical scenes shown on silver cup from Traprain Law*. Curle, 1923

damaged nature of some of the fonts might even be put forward as an argument for the destruction of the tanks by pagans in the process of destroying a Christian site, possibly during a postulated late fourth-century pagan revival. However, such an interpretation ignores the clear evidence for the deposition of sets of Christian pewter ware, in exactly the same type of contexts as the non-Christian pewter ware hoards, with no evidence that they had been destroyed or damaged in any way (**64**). In these hoards the Christian vessels were treated with as much respect as the putative pagan hoards.

At Appleshaw (Hants.) excavations in the nineteenth century uncovered 32 pewter vessels placed in a pit inserted through the floor of a villa. One of the vessels had a large Constantinian *chi-rho* on the base, and another dish was engraved with a fish symbol. From the Roman small town at Heybridge (Essex) a large hoard of pewter was found in a well of late Roman date; Nina Crummy has noted that one of the objects was decorated with a *chi-rho* symbol. Another pewter hoard with probable Christian associations comes from the Isle of Ely. A pewter bowl from Sutton, almost certainly part of the hoard also had a Constantinian *chi-rho* between A and Ω. A *chi-rho* was also found inscribed on the deliberately buried pewter vessel at Caerwent. Another possible ritual river find was a pewter bowl or dish bearing a *chi-rho* found on the bed of the Old Welney River (Cambs.).

A more ambiguously Christian pewter hoard is from Appleford (Oxon). Twenty-four pewter vessels were found in a deep well or shaft. A Christian identity for the collection of vessels has not been put forward before. However, there are two elements of the decoration which may be overtly Christian. The first is a possible *iota chi* cut into the base of a cast fluted bowl. More convincingly, a flat plate is decorated with an incised cross pattée. A similar cross was found carved on the back of a pewter dish from Boltisham Lode. The Appleford hoard is also important for the graffiti inscribed on another large plate, which reads: EMITA PARTA SVA LOVERNIANVS DONAVIT, which has been translated as 'Lovernianus presented the things he had bought'. This inscription is clearly significant if the hoard is interpreted as votive. It also brings to mind the inscriptions from the Christian silver hoard from Water Newton.

This brings us to a consideration of the find location of the precious Christian treasures discussed above. Water Newton, in Cambridgeshire, is in the heartland of the distribution of both pewter hoards and lead tanks. Again this area is where most of the precious metal hoards from late Roman Britain are found, especially if the clearly distinct hoards of probable looted treasure found just outside the province, such as Balline (Co. Limerick), Ballinrees (Co. Derry) and Traprain Law are ignored.

Historical reasons have been produced to explain the burial of some of these hoards. Catherine Johns, arguing for a pagan origin for the Thetford treasure, related the deposition to the anti-pagan decrees of the 390s, whilst Kenneth Painter argued that the Water Newton hoard was hidden to keep it from Roman robbers or by the robbers themselves. However, it is surely more than coincidental that these hoards were found in the very areas that the ritual pewter hoards were so predominantly found.

A final similarity between the deposition of pewter hoards and the deposition of Christian lead tanks can be seen in the presence of accompanying hoards of iron objects found with both types of deposit. At Icklingham the lead tank found in 1971 was accompanied by a large quantity of iron objects, and an iron object was found with pewter hoards from nearby. Large quantities of iron objects were also found with the possible Christian pewter hoard from Appleford, including 1.4m of iron chain, an iron steelyard and a scythe blade. At Stanwick (Northants.) the hoard of four pewter vessels in a pit was found just to the north of a hoard of iron objects. The distribution of iron hoards clearly overlapped with the distribution of pewter hoards and Christian lead tanks.

A consideration of these hoards and the inscriptions found on the Water Newton hoard make it clear that the deposition of hoard for votive purposes and the ritual dedication of vessels, whether made of pewter or silver, was not incompatible with Christianity. Indeed the votive plaques from Water Newton are merely Christian examples of the pagan tradition of using such plaques known from a number of sites in Britain. In late Roman Britain the rite of making votive offerings of vessels in watery and other contexts was an expression of religious belief common to both pagans and Christians. In this context the deposition of Christian lead tanks in such contexts takes on a new level of meaning.

Icklingham: a Christian landscape

The broad similarity in the geographical distribution of Christian lead tanks and pewter hoards can also be seen at a very local level in the area

64 *Map of pewter hoards, iron hoards and lead tanks in Britain*

surrounding the small Romano-British site at Icklingham (Suffolk). This site is best known for the possible Christian church (Building B) and the tile-built baptistery or font base to its east. These were adjacent to 41 inhumations, of which only one had evidence for any grave-goods. The Christian identity of the site rests primarily on the presence of the remains of at least four lead tanks from the immediate area, three of which had *chi-rho* inscriptions. There was also undoubtedly domestic activity in the area, with scatters of pottery in the field adjacent to the 'church' site, and occupation scatters on the opposite bank of the River Lark, and a building with a hypocaust was found about 200m to the north-west.

The earliest recorded lead tank from Icklingham was found during ploughing in 1726/7. A second tank found in 1932 probably came from the north-east side of Horsland Field, 200 to 300m north-east of the excavated site. This was decorated with *chi-rho* symbols between a reversed A and W. The third tank was found in 1971 probably near the site of the baptistery. This tank was filled with a large deposit of iron objects including hinges, nails and two saws, as well as cakes of lead and the lug of a fourth lead tank. This hoard of iron objects immediately brings to mind the iron-work hoard found with the Appleford pewter hoard.

The tanks and the iron-work hoard are, however, not the only unusual deposits to be found at Icklingham; fewer than four pewter hoards are known from the parish (**65**). The earliest found in 1839 at an unknown site contained nine vessels. In 1853 the British museum purchased a further 18 vessels from a second hoard, with the four vessels from the same hoard being bought by the Ipswich museum. In 1956 a third hoard of nine pewter vessels and a saw blade was found on high land to the north of the site. One of the objects from this hoard was decorated with a fish, similar to that found on the pewter dish from Sutton (Cambs.) a common symbol of Christianity. A fourth small hoard was found on the western edge of the parish in 1962, which consisted of a bronze bowl, a pewter platter and a pottery bowl.

There is also evidence for a third form of ritual deposition, the placement of coin hoards. At least five such hoards are known from Icklingham. The earliest recorded came from the villa site in 1877 on the northern corner of a wall in Room 3. It consisted of 33 bronze coins. In 1877, a second hoard was found to the north of the site in a small vase; it consisted of around 400 silver coins dating from Constantius II to Honorius. The next three come from unrecorded contexts. One found in 1902 in an earthenware bowl comprised 1064 coins dating up to Honorius, a fourth consisting of 12 radiate *minimi* and a fifth found in 1906 containing coins from Claudius II to Valentinian. Other scatters of coins have been found in the same field as the church site, and the fields to the north and south.

Another example of ritual deposition comes from the site itself. Before the construction of the church there was little activity on the site. The notable

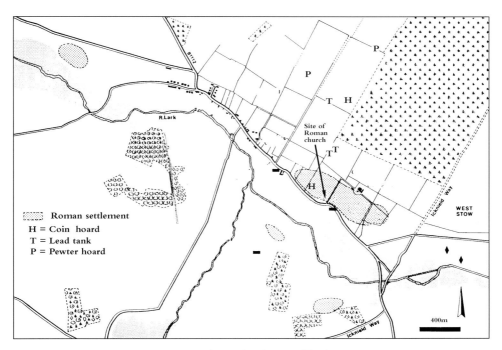

65 *Map showing hoarding in Icklingham*

exception was a large pit F32 close to the area where the church was later built. This feature was 3.8m in diameter and 2.45m deep. It seems to have been backfilled in a single event. The contents of this pit are extremely unusual. Most striking was a group of six skulls, including one child's. Unusual architectural fragments were also found in it: a complete limestone pillar (1.17m long) and fragments of unusual indented and grooved decorative roof-tiles.

A final less-understood example of probable ritual deposition from Icklingham takes the form of an assemblage of masks and statuettes, known as the 'Icklingham Bronzes' found in the area. Unfortunately, these were metal-detector finds looted from the site and illegally exported to the USA. Their precise context is unknown, but they appear to be a clear indication of an early Roman religious focus in the locality. Interestingly, the similar Willingham Fen of early Roman bronze figures and cult equipment was also found extremely close to a Late Roman lead font.

The focus of ritual deposits appears to spread beyond the parish of Icklingham itself (**66**). Three pewter hoards were found in the parish of Hockwold-cum-Wilton around 10 miles to the north, with others in the surrounding area. Hockwold is also the site of an important hoard of early Roman vessels. Mildenhall is only 4 miles to the north-west of Icklingham and Thetford is 10 miles to the north-east. Other hoards of early Roman vessels are found at Brandon (ten miles away) and possibly Santon Downham (12 miles away). A set of Iron Age religious equipment was found just across the River Lark at Cavenham, only around a mile distant.

Icklingham is the centre of a large number of unusual deposits, including lead tanks, iron-work, pewter vessels and coin hoards. Whilst, individually, the deposits are not unusual, the sheer quantity points to a large amount of ritual behaviour in the area. The unusual architectural fragments in pit F37 may relate to a focal pre-Christian religious structure, but the wider distribution of the deposits around the parish suggest that such votive activities were carried out throughout the surrounding landscape. At first it might appear that the pagan practice of ritual deposition throughout the landscape was replaced by a specific Christian focus of activity. However, if the chronology of the hoards is looked at, the matter is not so clear. The 'Icklingham Bronzes' can probably be dated to the first or second century AD, but this is the only deposit that must be dated to this period. All the other deposits fit better in a late Roman, indeed a later fourth-century context. The most easily datable deposits, the coin hoards, mostly belong to the later fourth century, with coin series extending up to Theodosius and Honorius. Although the only datable coin from the 1877 hoard was early, the context of the find in the ruins of the stone 'villa' structure suggests a later Roman date. It is harder to date the pewter hoards, but in such hoards elsewhere they mainly date to the fourth century, and are common in the late fourth century. Finally, the lead tanks themselves all date to the second half of the fourth century, as does the construction of

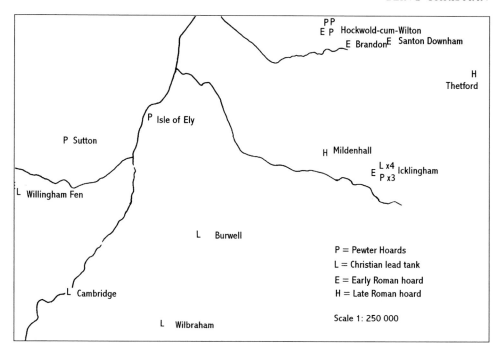

66 *Map showing hoarding in Icklingham region*

the church and baptistery (Phase III) with which they are probably contemporarily dated.

This suggests that, surprisingly, the high-point of deposition of ritual objects, especially lead and pewter vessels and tanks, appears to belong to the period *after* the construction of the church and baptistery and the destruction of any earlier temple. Although there was a clear pre-fourth-century tradition of votive deposition, the peak of such deposits comes after the introduction of Christianity into the area. The deposition of the lead tanks, the Christian element to the Mildenhall and Thetford hoards and the presence of a Christian fish-symbol on one of the pewter hoards all suggest that these deposits were not being placed by pagans in reaction to Christians, but by Christians themselves. For fourth-century Christians in Roman Britain the placement of ritual hoards was as natural as celebrating mass or carrying out baptisms; it was merely one of the options open to them as a means of expressing their beliefs.

The deposition of Roman Christian lead tanks can be seen to be just one thread in a widely practised late Roman tradition of votive deposition, including the placement of hoards of pewter vessels, many decorated with *chi-rho* symbols, and precious metal hoards, again often with a Christian element. Traditionally the placement of such deposits has been seen as an essentially pagan practice not carried out by Christians. This has led to the suggestion that the placement of lead tanks in such contexts was carried out by pagans as a form of symbolic destruction. However, the presence of *chi-rho* symbols on pewter hoards and on precious metal deposits would instead indicate that these hoards are as likely to be placed by Christians themselves. The lead tanks are perhaps best seen merely as a specialist form of pewter vessel, part of a range of such objects used for hoarding practices.

By appreciating that the lead tanks were objects worthy of votive deposition, we are adding another layer of understanding to their role. This is not to argue that they were not used for baptism, but that they had a more complex life history. In the same way that it has been suggested some of the pewter hoards were never intended to be used but merely to be placed in ritual deposits, the ritual deposition of the lead tank may have viewed as part of their destiny from the very beginning. The placement in a ritual deposit may have always been their destination. This may explain why several sites, such as Bourton-on-the-Water, Ashton and Icklingham have produced several tanks. They may not have been used simultaneously, but in series, each never having been intended to be used more than once or twice. In Roman military contexts altars were ritually disposed of through burial in the ground, and it may have been the correct way of disposing of sacred objects. Indeed in Lincolnshire fonts were disposed off through burial in the ground into the medieval period, in a tradition that clearly had a long ancestry in that part of England.

It is wrong to suggest that the deposition of Christian objects in such a manner is an example of absorption of pagan rites into the religion, and that those who carried them out were knowingly behaving in a pagan manner. Those who buried lead tanks in fourth-century Lincolnshire are as likely to have seen themselves as good Christians as those who buried fonts in four-teenth-century Lincolnshire. The issue of the deposition of objects in votive contexts is more likely to be such a basic way of expressing religious belief that it was seen as neither pagan nor Christian. After all, just because pre-Christian religious believers prayed does not mean that the act of prayer in Christianity is pagan; it is merely an established mode of religious practice.

Conclusions

For many inhabitants of Roman Britain, both pagan and Christian, their most frequent contact with the Church would not have been when celebrating the Eucharist on Sundays, but in the mundane encounters with Christian symbolism that must have taken place on a daily basis. The appearance of the *chi-rho* symbol on coinage, official regalia and in other administrative contexts would have served to constantly link the Church and the state in the minds of the subjects of the Empire. Although the *chi-rho* was undoubtedly used as symbol of Imperial power, it retained its religious meaning, and was frequently used in purely ecclesiastical contexts. Christian imagery was found in a wide range of contexts, public, private, and official. Apart from the use of the *chi-rho* Christians were still exploring the various ways in which their belief could be visually communicated. Some, such as the aristocratic and educated villa owners chose to explore their faith through complex allegorical art intimately linked to pre-existing classical modes of expression. For them Christianity did not require a rejection of forms of knowledge and culture that would later be labelled pagan. Elsewhere, the placement of Christian objects in votive contexts and the ceremonies that might have surrounded this also showed strong links with pre-existing pagan practices. However, at this early stage there is no reason to believe these practices were understood as being distinctly non-Christian. What we see in Roman Britain are early Christians attempting to make sense of their new religion and express their beliefs in ways which they saw as culturally appropriate. In both cases it would only be later changes in religious dogma that would condemn these modes of worship. As we have already seen when exploring the forms of early churches, the Christian communities were still striving to define the parameters of their ritual and material behaviour as much as their theological beliefs. This continuing quest to define what constituted 'Christian' ritual practices runs through many aspects of the archaeology of Romano-British Christiantiy, including art, and as we shall see in the next chapter, burials.

6

DYING CHRISTIAN

For Christians, perhaps more than any of the other religions of the Roman world, death was not the end but the beginning. The transition from this world to the next was believed to be a move from the torments and travails of this earthly life to the paradise of the hereafter. This meant that, in theory, death and burial should be something to be celebrated rather than a period of sadness. For believers it was understood that their real death occurred in baptism, when their old life died and they were reborn again through Jesus. Death was thus simply the completion of a journey towards redemption begun in baptism.

However, despite these broad beliefs the theological complexities of death and dying had not been defined in detail. Concepts that were intimately associated with death in the Middle Ages, such as purgatory, had failed to develop in the third and fourth centuries. Although the ultimate destination of the soul of the departed was heaven, this final transition did not take place until judgement day, as laid out in the apocalyptic Book of Revelations. In the meantime the souls were believed to reside in a kind of limbo state. It is important to understand that at this time Christians did not believe that the dead and living had the intimate relationship which developed in the Western Church in the medieval period. Although, as we shall see below, there were certain categories of special dead, the martyrs, who could intercede for the living, there was no belief that the living could intercede for the dead. It was believed that the destination of the soul was already decided at the point of death. There was no need for the community of the living to try and affect the path of the departed.

Although the destination of the soul was deemed most important, some early Christians also believed that the body of the dead would also rise. Some early Christian writers and teachers, such as Justin Martyr taught that bodily resurrection would occur, with the implication that the body of the dead must be preserved as much as possible. This belief may be reflected in attempts by early martyrs to ensure that their bodies were buried correctly, and bids by the authorities to ensure that this was not the case. However, the cases of the complete destruction of the bodies of martyrs tell us more about what the persecuting authorities perceived Christian belief to be, than what they themselves believed. Many early Christian writers, such as Tertullian, wrote in favour of bodily resurrection. He wrote in *De Resurrectione Caro* (On the Resurrection of the Body) that God would reconstitute the corpses of the dead and even make wild animals vomit up the bones of people they had eaten. However, others taught the opposite, and that the new home for the soul would be a spiritual body, not its physical container from its sojourn in this world. Ultimately, Christian theology on this point appears confused and contradictory.

For the dying Christian the preparations for the next world began before death. As we have seen, many Christians were not baptized until the end of their lives, thus when death was impending it was ensured that the dying person had been admitted fully into the Church. This would have been a simple ceremony; the patient would have made a confession of faith, they would then be sprinkled with holy water and anointed with holy oil in the sign of the cross. Once this was done, the focal point of the death ritual was the giving of the Eucharist to the dying individual. This was a sign that they were full members of the Christian Church. In some parts of the Empire it was even given to corpses. It was sometimes also given as part of the ceremony of deathbed forgiveness. Unlike later rites of penance the early Christian rites could not be repeated, so many Christians did not seek forgiveness until their deathbeds. The ceremony involved a simple act of confession, the person then entered a state of penitence, they were then reconciled with the Church by taking the Eucharist, and sometimes by a laying on of hands.

Although the actual texts for the ceremonies around the deathbed and grave have not survived, scholars have reconstructed the Late Roman rituals for death and burial, the *Ordo defunctorum*, from later manuscript sources. In this simple liturgy, once death had occurred the prayers and a psalm (Ps.113) were said, followed by an antiphon. The corpse was then washed and placed on a bier. More prayers followed, including another antiphon and a further psalm. The body was then carried to the church to the accompaniment of further psalms and antiphons. This procession was an important part of the ceremony. In many ways it paralleled the Roman ceremony of *adventus*, the triumphant entry of victorious emperors and generals, only in this case it celebrated the entrance of the dead person's soul into the afterlife. Once it was in the church a vigil occurred, with prayers for the soul until burial had taken place. This vigil might also include readings from the Book of Job. Finally, the body was buried, accompanied by further prayers and psalms. Interestingly, this early liturgy does not stipulate that a funerary mass has to be said.

This reconstructed liturgy may help us to understand better the religious structure of Christian funerals, but it is important to remember that whatever the theological and spiritual elements of the death of a person, these are not the only factors that come into play. The personal sense of grief and loss felt by the family and friends of the dead individual and their social role in wider society are just some of the other influences that may have influenced the funeral rites. When it comes to planning the funeral and burial, religion may in fact be one of the least important things taken into consideration. Although we have become accustomed to seeing a funeral as a purely religious occasion, we know that this may not always have been the case. An incident from the life of St Martin of Tours written not long after his death in AD 397 gives us an intriguing insight into the way in which the Church in Western Gaul viewed funeral rites in the late fourth century:

> XII.(1) It happened during the following period that while he was on a journey he came across the corpse of a pagan which was being carried out for burial in accordance with superstitious funeral rites. Seeing in the distance a crowd of people coming towards him, he stopped for a while, not knowing what it was. For he was about five hundred paced away so it was difficult to make out what he was seeing. (2) However, because he could see a group of peasants and the linen cloths laid over the corpse fluttering in the wind, he thought that they were performing, pagan sacrificial rites, for it was the custom for peasants of Gaul, in their pitiable delusions, to carry demonic representations, covered with a white veil, over their fields. (3) And so Martin raised his hand and made the sign of the cross against those who were coming towards him. He ordered the crowd to stop and to set down what they were carrying. And now you would have seen an amazing thing. These miserable people first became rigid like rocks; (4) then, when they made a great effort to move forward, they found that they were unable to move any further and went spinning round in a ridiculous whirling movement until they were overcome with dizziness and set down the burden of the corpse. They looked round at each other in amazement, wondering in silence what had happened (5) But when the holy man understood that these people had gathered for a funeral, **not for a religious ceremony** [author's emphasis], he raised his hand once more and granted them the power to depart and to carry the corpse.

> *Life of St Martin of Tours* (trans. Caroline White)

Martin of Tours was notorious for his direct action against pagan religious practices. If even he believed that a funeral was not a religious ceremony we need to be careful when exploring the relationship between burial rites and religious belief.

In general, archaeologists have become split into two camps when assessing the Christianity or otherwise of Roman burials of this period. On one hand, there are those who believe that Christian burials are always aligned west–east, laid out lengthways in the grave and accompanied by no artefacts that might be interpreted as grave-goods. It is this broad burial rite that emerges in the medieval world as typical of Christian death rituals. On the other hand, many archaeologists will point out burials in the Roman world that despite being certainly Christian, are either of the wrong alignment, in the wrong position or accompanied by grave-goods, and maintain that it is impossible to recognise a Christian grave in Roman Britain. As is usual in such cases, both sides have valid points, but equally they have their weaknesses. As with all aspects of the study of Christianity in this period, the problem is that it is in this period that the practices which later became embedded in tradition in the later Church are only just beginning to be consolidated. In reality the burial rite is in flux. It is clear that many of the cluster of elements that would characterise Christian burials could be found in pagan graves or were missing from Christian graves, but equally it is clear that by the mid-fifth century AD a clearly Christian burial rite had evolved and was used across what was left of the Roman Empire and beyond, though with the expected regional variations. Rather than merely attempting to recognise elements of this burial rite in the third and fourth century we instead need to explore why these elements became to be characterised as Christian.

Death and burial in Roman Britain

Rather than looking for individual aspects of the late Roman burial rite in Britain that might be considered Christian, it is necessary to consider these traditions in their wider context. As might be expected, the burial traditions of Roman Britain are a complex mix of native rites and new introductions from elsewhere in the Roman Empire. Strong regional variations are also visible across the country. Relatively little is known about how the native Iron Age tribes disposed of their dead, with a few notable exceptions. In the late Iron Age in much of Britain the dead are simply missing from the archaeological record. The use of the burial mounds of earth and stone which were so common in much of Bronze Age Britain had declined, except in a few upland areas. Instead the dead were disposed of in a way which seems to have left few physical remains. It is possible that they may have been cremated and their ashes scattered. Occasionally, local traditions can be recognised. For example, across much of Wessex, body parts and the bodies of babies are sometimes found in the bottom of storage pits. However, they clearly only represent a minority of the dead in this area, and is probably part of a wider fertility ritual. Elsewhere, in Dorset and the south-west a burial tradition was used, and the dead were placed in stone-lined graves.

The most distinct changes came in the south-east of Britain, in the areas closest to the Continent. In the years between the first invasion of Britain by

Julius Caesar in 53 BC and the second invasion under Claudius there was a transformation of burial rites. Cremations, usually accompanied by large quantities of imported pottery, become increasingly common on both sides of the Thames. Limited to the north of the Thames a number of very wealthy cremations are also found. These new cremation rites are all very similar to the burial rites found in Northern Gaul, and probably reflect increasing interaction between the native elites of Britain and the Continent. At a wider level, this practice of cremations accompanied by pottery vessels and other grave-goods reflects the prevailing tradition found across much of the Western Roman Empire. With the advent of permanent Roman control in the mid-first century AD this burial rite became widespread across much of lowland Britain. Although we can see a major change in the burial rite, there is no reason to link it to a change in religious practice. Although, not surprisingly many Roman gods and goddesses became integrated into native British religious practices there is no evidence in any sense of a fundamental change of religion in Britain. The reasons for the change in burial are far more complex than this. It is undoubtedly tied up with wider shifts in the way late Iron Age and Romano-British society operated. The pressures of a political threat, territorial takeover and new government as well as shifts in the way in which the native British identified themselves are equally if not more important. This is not the place to begin a detailed exploration of early Roman burial practices, but one simple lesson needs to be brought forward into any discussion of later changes in burial practice. A change in burial practice is not necessarily a reflection of a change in religion, and many other factors may come into play.

Following the expansion of the rite of cremation in the first and second centuries AD there was a second major change in burial rites in the third and fourth centuries. Britain saw a shift from cremation being the predominant tradition to inhumation. Again, as with cremation, this pattern reflected wider changes in the Roman world. The move to burial of the entire body seems to have begun in Rome and spread outwards during the second century. By the mid-third century inhumation had replaced cremation as the main form of burial throughout most of the Empire, including Britain. The precise reason for this major change is still greatly debated, but once more it is clear that a simple mono-causal shift in religion is not satisfactory. It is certainly much too early to have been caused by the increasing popularity of Christianity.

As with the cremation rite, the inhumation burial rite in Britain showed an immense amount of variation. In the third and fourth centuries people could be buried in stone, lead or wooden coffins in a range of alignments. The body might be laid out full-length, in a crouched position or even face down. Grave-goods might be completely absent or include high-class glass, pottery vessels and personal items. However, despite this huge range of alternatives found in the graves of late Roman Britain the German archaeologist Lucas Quensel-von Kalbern feels that it is possible to recognise two broad traditions. One class of burials tend to be mainly aligned west-east and the bodies are usually laid out on their backs. grave-goods are rarely found. Amongst this type, the graves are often protected by the presence of a stone or tile lining. It also often includes the graves of very young children. These burials stand in contrast to burials which are more likely to be north-south in alignment with the body placed in a wide range of positions. A range of grave-goods is also found. A number of unusual practices exist amongst a minority of these burials. The most notable of these is the practice of decapitating the body after death and placing the head in the grave, either in its correct anatomical position or elsewhere.

Another important distinction between these two burial rites is their internal organisation. Burials of the first group are often laid out neatly in rows, usually running north-south. The graves show little evidence of inter-cutting, instead the individual graves clearly respect each other. These cemeteries have been termed 'managed cemeteries' by Charles Thomas. They contrast with burials from the second group, which often show different patterns of organisation. For example, groups of such burials may often cluster around a central burial. In general, less emphasis is placed on the overall layout of the cemetery. Instead organisation and careful consideration of their physical relationship occurs at the level of individual clusters of graves. These patterns are not completely exclusive; in some cases cemeteries with graves which belong primarily to the first group and contain mainly well-ordered graves also include one or two clusters of graves in the second group.

This can be seen at the cemetery at Poundbury, Dorchester (**67**). This cemetery is of great importance in the study of Roman burial practice in Britain. Standing between the River Frome and a main road leading north-west from the town of *Durnovaria*, over 1,400 burials were found during archaeological investigations between 1964 and 1980. Although a few Late Iron Age and Early Roman burials were discovered, most of the graves belong to the Late Roman period. The main body of the burials in the cemetery consisted of a group of around 1,100 burials aligned west-east. Most of these were buried in wooden coffins and gravegoods were largely absent. A number of burials were also buried in lead-lined or stone coffins. Included in this main group were the remains of at least eight stone built mausolea, decorated internally with painted plaster. These graves were well organised in north-south rows. Even the mausolea were integrated into this overall plan.

Around the edges of this central cemetery, however, a number of different groups of graves could be recognised. Some, such as the graves to the east of the main cemetery were aligned north-south and contained many gravegoods. Gravegoods were also common in the west-east aligned graves to the north of the main site, and in a number of other peripheral grave groups. To the south-west a number of roughly rectangular ditched enclosures were recorded. Unlike the mausolea, which contained several burials, possibly family groups, these enclosures contained only one central grave. In this they have stronger parallels with the ditched enclosures from the Lankhills cemetery at Winchester. Here, the central graves contained burials accompanied by high-status, and probably official, belt sets.

Whilst it is clear that the two Late Roman burial traditions are fairly distinct, we need to explore in more detail precisely what the implications are. It is tempting to leap to the conclusion that one group, that of west-east burials, is the burials of Christians and the other is of pagans. However, as we have already seen, a change in burial rites does not automatically reflect changes in religious beliefs.

We can perhaps begin our further investigation of these burials by looking at their spatial distribution, at several levels of resolution. Looking at their national distribution, it is clear that both types of burial are found widely spread across the country. Both types are more common in the lowland area of Britain, running approximately south of the line from the Severn estuary to the Humber. However, there are notable outliers of both types around the major Roman towns and military settlements to the north of this area, such as Chester and York. They are also both found at all types of settlement, including major towns, small towns and villas. The fact that the two types of burial are not regionally mutually exclusive shows that explanations based on regional identity or local custom are not likely. More information about the relationship between these two burial rites can be gleaned by exploring their physical relationship at a more local level.

At a local level the two burial groups often appear to have been contemporary. For example, at Ilchester (Somerset) a large cemetery to the north-east of the town at Northover appears to have been a well-organised burial site containing predominantly west-east aligned graves with few, if any, grave-goods (**68**). Several lead and carved stone coffins have been recovered from this site. Meanwhile, to the south-east of the town, graves have been found running along the two main roads out of the town in this direction. Amongst burials from this site those at Little Spittle have been excavated. These were shown to lie amidst a series of enclosures in which roadside buildings had stood earlier. These burials followed the alignments of the existing enclosures. Some of the graves contained objects, such as coins, knives, bracelets or hobnailed boots. The bodies were laid out in a range of positions; some were crouched and others were decapitated. The only indications of coffins were iron nail or slight soil marks indicating that they had been wooden, in contrast to the lead and stone ones found at Northover. The evidence from the objects in these graves suggests that they were at least fourth century, and probably mid- or late fourth-century in date.

A similar pattern of the two burial rites existing at the same time can also be seen at nearby Shepton Mallet. Here, excavations have shown the two different burial traditions in operation in adjacent enclosures (**69**).

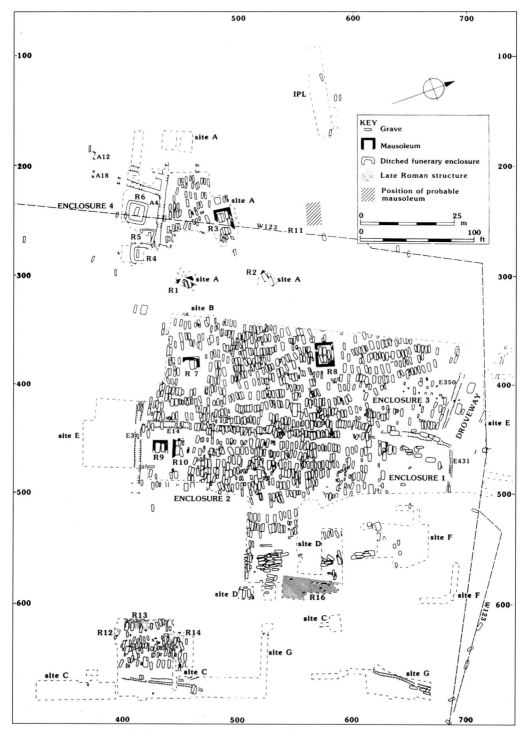

67 *The late roman cemetery at Poundbury, Dorchester (Dorset)*

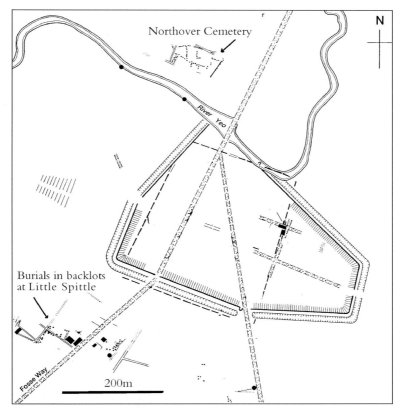

68 *Map of Ilchester showing location of Roman burials at Little Spittle and Northover*

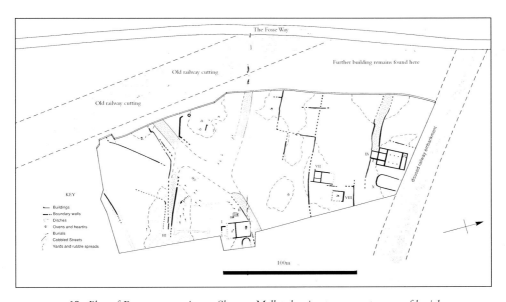

69 *Plan of Roman occupation at Shepton Mallet showing two separate areas of burial*

The main group consisted of 17 burials aligned west-east; one burial in this group was placed in a lead coffin. However, elsewhere the burials were placed on a north-south alignment, some were buried face down and others were decapitated. The burials of this small community were split roughly equally between the two rites, which may have implications for the number of Christians in the locality.

This pattern is not limited to the south-west of England. A similar situation has been found at Ashton (Northants). Again there is a formal cemetery of west-east burials, which stands to the south-west of the town (**70**). Over 170 graves have been identified, and they indicate a high degree of organisation with the graves arranged in rows. The burials were laid out on their backs with no grave-goods, except two Constantinian coins associated with a young child. There were possible boundaries to the cemeteries to the east and north. There was skeletal evidence for the burial of children, infants and neonates. The dates for the cemetery are uncertain, but it seems to start some time in the early to mid-fourth century. Other burials, some decapitated and many with grave foods were found elsewhere in the town, but mainly associated with individual roadside properties and enclosures. This spatial separation of the two burial rites has even been found within the same cemetery. At Poundbury, burials containing such rites as decapitation and prone burial were placed in peripheral areas of the managed cemetery.

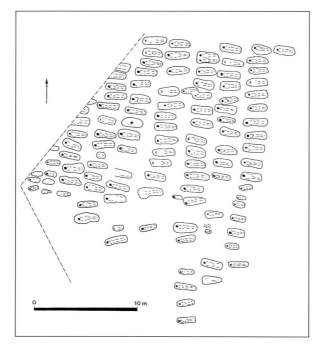

70 *The late Roman 'managed' cemetery at Ashton (Northants.)*

We can draw several conclusions from this pattern of burials. Firstly, that not only are the two types of burial broadly contemporary, but secondly that one or both of them demands that burials of the other kind should be spatially segregated. This contrasts with earlier Romano-British burial practices, where many different burial rites could exist side-by-side in a cemetery. There are also good reasons to believe that the followers of the tradition of west-east, findless graves may have been wealthier and had more political or social power than followers of the other rite. At cemeteries, such as Butt Road, Colchester and Poundbury, Dorset this tradition appears to have come to dominate an important pre-existing cemetery, rather than establishing a new burial ground.

At Butt Road, the cemetery stands to the south-west of the important Roman town of *Camulodunum* (**71**). In Period 1, phase 3, probably dating to the early fourth century AD, a cemetery of burials aligned north-south was laid out over a site where a number of even earlier burials, including some cremations, had been placed sometime between the end of the first century AD and the early third century AD. Just over half of these early fourth-century graves were accompanied by grave-goods, including pottery vessels, personal adornments, such as armlets, and shoes. A number of clusters of a graves could be recognised, and it was suggested that they may have been family groups.

Sometime between 320 and 340 the cemetery underwent a major reorganisation. Over 650 burials were placed in the new cemetery. Most were contained in timber coffins, though some were placed in lead coffins. The burials from this phase were uniformly arranged broadly west-east, in rough north-south rows. Unlike graves from the preceding period, very few grave-goods were found. To the northwest of the cemetery stood the probable church building discussed in chapter 3.

The followers of this rite had enough power to prevent or at least discourage a continuation of early burial rites, forcing people to either convert to the new rite or bury their dead in an alternative site. As we have seen from Ilchester and Ashton these alternate sites were often in less prime locations, reusing areas previously used for domestic occupation. Unlike the major burial sites, graves in these new cemeteries would not have enjoyed the clear prominence that the major, formal cemeteries had. Hints of a wealth differential can also be seen amidst the graves themselves. At Ilchester the expensive lead and stone coffins were only found in the Northover cemetery, and in Poundbury the lead coffins and stone mausolea decorated with painted plaster are clear indicators of wealth.

So far I have carefully avoided the question of the relationship between burial type and religious belief. It is of course tempting to argue that the west-east burial group is Christian. However, other suggestions have been made in the past. Two main reasons have been put forward for the late Roman 'managed cemetery'. The first suggestion is that the phenomenon reflects an increased interest in town councils and other local bodies in the spatial organisation of town planning. Unfortunately little evidence has been put forward to support this point of view. There is no epigraphic or textual evidence to suggest that there was an increased secular bureaucratisation or centralisation of burial rites. If anything the apparatus of local civic government was being weakened in the later Roman period. The change in the internal planning of Late Roman cities suggests that little interest was being taken in the management of space. Indeed, although some of the towns mentioned above would have had a town council, most of the small towns and rural sites are unlikely to have had any form of organised civic administration.

The other explanation for major changes in the organisation of cemeteries in the later Roman period is the increased power of the Church, following the Edict of Milan in AD 313. It has been suggested that influence of the Church combined with increased conversion to the religion lead to a Christianisation of the burial rite, which was reflected by the move to organised west-east cemeteries. However, this does not explain why Christian burials should automatically be aligned west-east or have fewer grave-goods. Most of the explanations given for these attributes, such as it was so the dead would be facing Jerusalem on Judgement Day, are not attested in contemporary writings and instead have the tang of *post-hoc* justifications.

To get a better feeling for the relationship between the growth of Christianity and these burial rites we need to consider the chronology in a little more detail. If either of these rites were Christian in origin we would expect to find very few examples of them until after AD 313. Before this date it is unlikely that followers of Christianity would have the social power needed to take over major cemeteries or set up important new burial sites. If, however, these traditions are earlier than this date, the situation is more complicated.

By their very nature the 'managed cemeteries' lacking grave-goods are difficult to date accurately. However, in some larger cemeteries such as Butt Road, Colchester and Poundbury it is possible to suggest a potential date. The transition to more organised, findless burials at Butt Road was dated by the excavators to between 320 and 340; at Poundbury the main phase of use appears to have begun in the early to mid fourth century. The slight evidence from Ashton and Ilchester suggest a mid fourth-century date. The dating evidence thus does broadly suggest a post-313 dating.

The move towards managed cemeteries can therefore clearly be seen to have probably begun after freedom of the Church. However, it is unlikely that the rapid expansion in the rite in the early to mid-fourth century was purely due to an increase in Christianity, suggesting the rite did not begin as a purely Christian tradition. In fact all the written evidence suggests that in the fourth century the Church had a fairly *laissez-faire* attitude to burial. As we have seen earlier, the theology of death and burial was fairly ill-developed and as even Augustine of Hippo noted in the *City of God*: 'Therefore, all such offices, that is, the care taken with funerals, the embalming for burial, the procession of the

71 *The plan of the late Roman cemetery at Butt Road, Colchester.* Crummy et al., 1993

mourners, are more for the comfort of the survivors than to assist the dead.' (*De Civ Dei* 1.13). He also wrote: 'Regardless of what is spent for burying the body it is not an aid to salvation but a duty of our humanity according to that love by which no one ever hated his own flesh' (*De Cura Gerenda Pro Mortuis* 18). For this leading churchman at least burial rites were more important for the bereaved than for the deceased. As such, it is not surprising that there was no strict dogma about funerary rituals.

We have a few other hints from Christian writers as to what a Christian burial might be expected to look like. They suggested that their practices were the same as those used on Jesus himself, essentially a continuation of traditional Jewish burial traditions. In general the evidence from early writers is vague and in places contradictory. Tertullian, writing in the early to mid-third century stated that the body should be laid in a tomb and anointed with spices. Minucius Felix, in his defence of Christianity *Octavius*, written around the same time or slightly after, suggested that wreaths and incense were forbidden (*Octavius* XII). It is not unjustified to say that placing the body in a tomb and anointing it with spices were practices applied to the majority of late Roman burials, and there is nothing diagnostically Christian about them. Importantly, the early authorities seem to mention no prescriptions against the inclusion of objects in the grave or demands for a west-east orientation. Perhaps, the only important stricture is that the body should not be cremated. Yet again, though, this also reflects contemporary shifting burial practices across the Empire.

However, we are still left with the conundrum that for some reason in the fourth century this pre-existing tradition of west-east organised cemeteries becomes increasingly popular, not just in Britain, but across most of the Roman Empire. In the few cemeteries where we can suggest a Christian identity for the departed for other reasons, such as Icklingham and St Paul-in-the-Bail, Lincoln, the graves all follow this tradition. If this burial rite is not Christian in itself, it is certainly the burial rite which Christians follow. But if there are no strong theological reasons why the Church should promote these burial rites there are perhaps more political and social reasons why it might be interested in encouraging a uniform burial rite, and it is possible to integrate the two suggested models for managed cemeteries to achieve a more rounded explanation for increased control of burial in the fourth century.

In the later Empire elite families were increasingly withdrawing from their roles in municipal government, as positions in the *ordo* went from being an honour (*honor*) to being a fiscal and legal burden (*munior*). With the reorganisation of Britain into four or five smaller provinces, and the presence of an imperial capital at Trier in nearby *Gallia Belgica*, these elites were closer to centralised imperial and bureaucratic sources of power. As we have seen the Church may have increasingly acted to the fill the void in municipal administration left by the changing role of the elites. Following the Edict of Milan the imperial service became increasingly Christianised, which would have encouraged local elites to convert, and the high profile of the Church in towns may also have encouraged conversion. It seems that, although there was an increased architectural investment on rural villas, members of the elite were still being buried in towns. This is reflected, on the one hand, by the lack of high-status burial sites associated with villa sites, though some mausolea such as those at Bancroft and Lullingstone are known, and on the other by the presence of high status burials from urban cemeteries such as Poundbury, York and London.

Peter Brown has suggested that in the fourth century the Church increasingly asserted control over burial rites to prevent high-status families using burial ritual as a focus of ostentatious display, jostling for power, both with other families, and the Church itself. Although as suggested by the Poundbury and Lankhills evidence the Church was not always able to prevent the expression of high-status through burials, and may even have allowed some such expression for pragmatic political reasons, in general this increased control over burial is reflected in the 'managed cemetery'. The concept of the unified kinship of the Church was played upon. The use of organised rows of burials prevented the clustering of individual burials in kin-groups. By ensuring such groups were spatially dispersed, it was possible in cemeteries to de-emphasise the role of families, and focus on the unifying power of the Church as a corporate body. Although, the Church did not invent the tradition of west-east burials with few grave-goods it appears to have taken it over, not from pure theological motives, but from the more pragmatic motives of power, control and prestige. The political power of the Church, even in Britain, would have given it the practical control over the urban cemeteries it needed to squeeze the non-orthodox burial rites to the margins. Conformity to this burial rite need not reflect conversion to Christianity, but it probably indicated a general accommodation with its increasing social power.

Those who refused to accept this development were forced to bury their dead elsewhere. In the case of the urban poor this meant converting derelict back lots into temporary cemeteries. The wealthy had the option of retreating to their rural estates and establishing or maintaining cemeteries there. The growth of increasingly unusual burial rites, such as decapitation, burial face down, other mutilation, and the increased placement of dead babies in unusual contexts, such as corn driers and storage pits may have in fact been a way of actively signalling a refusal to conform to this notionally Christian identity, by performing rites which actively indicated a disdain for the social norms.

So far this discussion has focused on general burial rites. That is general trends, which may or may not make attribution of a Christian identity to a cemetery more or less likely. However, there are cases where it might be possible to identify individual graves as Christians, irrelevant of their wider context. These include, gravestones and so-called 'plaster burials'.

Christian gravestones

The detailed exploration of Christian burial rites in Roman Britain is made complicated by a lack of the overtly Christian gravestones which are so widely spread elsewhere in the Empire. The use of stone grave monuments bearing carved epitaphs in Latin were just one of the many innovations to funerary rituals introduced into Britain by the Romans. The use of these gravestones, however, never seems to have really become popular amongst the native population. They are mostly found in the large suburban cemeteries around towns and the cemeteries close to military forts and their associated settlements. The names of many of those commemorated on these graves show that they were not of native British origin, but from elsewhere in the Empire. Although some British were provided with gravestones they seem to have been in the minority. The use of stone funerary monuments is much rarer in rural cemeteries, where we can assume that the communities were primarily British, and had fewer external influences.

Britain's failure to develop a sense of attachment to the use of gravestones reflects a wider failure to cultivate the use of all forms of monumental stone inscriptions. Although they are not uncommon in the first and second centuries there was a signal failure to develop what has been called the 'epigraphic habit'. This meant that the practice failed to continue into the third and fourth centuries AD.

Perhaps the most widely surviving examples of late Roman inscriptions in Britain are milestones. The number of gravestones that can be placed in the final two centuries of Roman rule is small, around 20 in total. One of the biggest challenges for exploring these late gravestones is how to date them. Unlike modern grave markers they do not include the date of birth or death of the deceased. Instead they have to be dated indirectly. The main way of dating the stones is by examining the shape of letters carved on them. In the first and second centuries most inscriptions were carved in Latin capitals familiar to us today. However, from the few datable inscriptions we do have, it is clear that letter shapes were changing. Malcolm Todd has argued that the letters A, F, G, L, M, N, R and S all showed particularly clear developments. Assuming that inscriptions using these later letter forms date to the mid-third century or later it is possible to recognize a small group of gravestones which may belong to the later Roman period (**72**).

Interestingly, these stones have an exclusively Northern distribution and are found along the course of Hadrian's Wall. The most distinctive is the gravestone of a Greek man Flavius Antigonas Papias which was found in the cemetery on the edge of Carlisle. It has been suggested that he may have been Christian (**73**). The inscription bears the formula *vixit plus minus* (he lived more or less) followed by his age, sixty. A similar use of *plus minus* also occurs on another stone from this group from Brougham (Northumberland), the site of the Roman fort of

72 *Distibution of probable Christian gravestones from Roman Britain*

Brocavum, which reads: *TITTUS M … VIXIT ANNIS PLVS MINVS XXXIII.* It has been argued that the use of this phrase indicates a lack of interest in mortal age that might be expected of a Christian. This phrase is widely found on Christian gravestones of late fourth-century and later date elsewhere in the Roman Empire, and Mark Handley has recorded its use on over 230 Christian gravestones from Gaul and Spain. The stone from Carlisle also includes the letters *DM*, which stand for *Dis Manibus* ('To the spirits of the departed') which is often assumed to be indicative of a pagan identity. However, this phrase is widely found on clearly Christian gravestones from across the western Roman Empire. It is even found on a probable post-Roman gravestone from Tomen-y-Mur in Wales. Handley has also suggested that the term *titulum posuit* ('placed this tomb or memorial'), used on some late Roman graves in Britain, may have reflected a Christian identity. It occurred on seven gravestones from Britain, again all in the north of Britain. Like the other possible Christian phrases it is widely used on Christian gravestones, particularly in Trier.

Another possible Christian burial inscription comes from York, carved onto the side of a stone coffin rather than an upstanding tombstone. This small child's coffin was found to the south-west of the railway station in part of a well-known cemetery. The touching inscription reads:

> To the spirits of the departed (and) of Simplicia Florentina, a most innocent soul, who lived ten months, her father, Felicius Simplex, made this: (soldier) of the Sixth Legion Victrix.

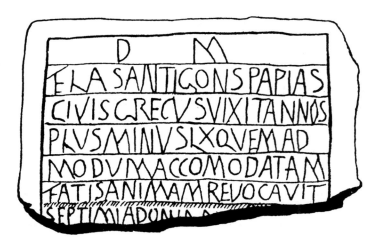

73 *The gravestone of Antigonas Papias from Carlisle*

Although there are no overt signs of Christianity, it may have been a Christian burial. The phrase 'innocent soul' (anime innocentissime) implies an interest in the concept of the soul, and the name Simplicia was also a popular one amongst early Christians. However, it would be stretching the evidence to argue that this stone is definitely Christian, and it can only be considered as a 'possibility'.

The other members of this group are different in some ways to the Carlisle and York stones as they are more crudely carved. They are carved onto rough slabs of stone rather than the more finely worked shape of the traditional Roman gravestone. The epitaphs are quite simple giving only the name and age, but little else. There is a noticeable lack of any overt reference to pagan religious beliefs, such as the use of the *DM* abbreviation or mention of the known pagan traditions of the afterlife. Even the names given are simple, consisting of just one name rather than the more usual three-part Latin name. Several of these names such as *Tancorix* on the stone from Old Carlisle end in the element *−rix* meaning 'kingly'. Other examples of such names are unknown from other Roman gravestones, but are found on some firmly Christian early medieval gravestones from Northern Britain and Wales. Even though some of these graves lack the overt Christian phrases explored above, they are so similar in location and form that a Christian identity seems likely. They are also very similar to several clearly Christian gravestones dating from the early to mid-fifth century.

A final example of a possible Christian gravestone from the northern frontier also comes from Maryport, though unlike those discussed so far it has no inscription. This fragment of a stone plaque has a *chi-rho* carved onto it instead (**74**). Unfortunately this tantalising piece of stone has now been

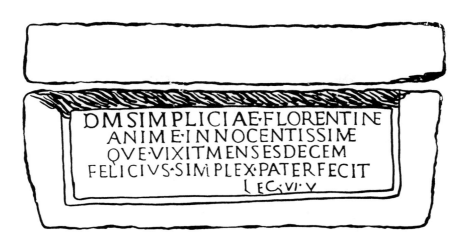

74 *The stone coffin of Simplicia Florentina (York)*

75 *Late Roman gravestones. (Top left) Brougham (Cumbria); (top right) Maryport (Cumbria); (bottom left) Old Carlisle (Cumbria); (bottom right) Maryport (Cumbria)*

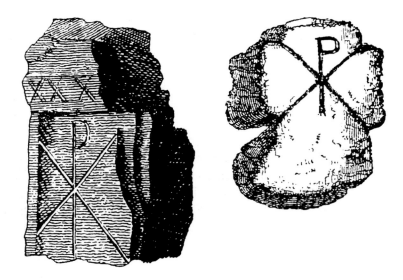

76 Chi-rho *symbols carved on the stone. (left) Maryport (Cumbria) (right) St Just (Cornwall)*

lost. It is probably from a tombstone, though without any inscription this cannot be proved. However, unlike the rough stone inscriptions already mentioned this is clearly from a well-carved object, and is clearly integrated into its formal design. There are no other parallels to this object from Britain and it is the only definitely Roman example of a *chi-rho* carved onto stone. Another carved *chi-rho* stone was found at St Just (Cornwall), again using this later form of *chi-rho* (**76***)*. However, this piece comes from an area where there are no recorded Roman inscriptions, but good evidence for fifth- and sixth-century Christian stones, and it too probably belongs to this period. Whilst the Maryport *chi-rho* must remain poorly understood, it does at least add circumstantial evidence to the possibility of the other gravestones from Maryport and nearby being Christian.

Although this number of late Roman and probably Christian gravestones is small compared with the numbers found on the Continent, the overall distribution of inscriptions over time is similar. Mark Handley has pointed out that the chronological spread of inscriptions in Britain is identical to that found on the Continent, following what has become known as the 'Mrozek Curve'. This shows an increase in the number of inscriptions until around AD 200 followed by a rapid decrease until the end of the third century AD. There was then a rise in the use of inscriptions in the later fourth and fifth centuries AD. This pattern of rise, fall and rise again in inscription numbers is exactly that seen in Britain. After the paucity of fourth-century gravestones, there is a resurgence in the number of inscriptions, with over 250 inscribed gravestones dating to the fifth to seventh centuries. The paucity of Christian gravestones in late Roman Britain cannot thus be read as a reflection of the absolute level of Christianity in Britain in the fourth century; it merely shows that late Roman Britain followed the same broad trends in the use of inscriptions as the rest of the Roman Empire.

Plaster burials

It has been argued that as the body in the grave of Simplicia Florentina was set in gypsum that this was also a reason to argue for a Christian identification. This was one of a group of burials from Late Roman Britain that are marked out by the fact that the body has been covered in a layer of plaster, gypsum or quicklime. The bodies have usually been wrapped in a shroud; sometimes this can still be seen imprinted in the plaster. They are then always placed in a lead or stone coffin before the plaster is added. It has sometimes been suggested that this practice might be an indication of Christianity, as it was thought that the 'plaster' might help preserve the bodies, reflecting a wider interest in preventing the corruption of the body until it rose on Judgement Day. However, this belief holds little water. Firstly, although plaster and gypsum may preserve the body, the use of quicklime, such as found in a grave (Gr.687) from Butt Road, Colchester, would actually hasten the decomposition of the corpse. Secondly, there are too many examples of 'plaster' burials occurring in clearly pagan graves. For example, the burial from Butt Road was from Period 1, Phase 3 dating to c.AD 300-c.320; it did not belong to the later possible Christian cemetery. 'Plaster' burials did undoubtedly spread in popularity during the third and fourth centuries AD, and in some cases it has been found in clearly Christian locations, such as the church of St Matthias at Trier and the martyrium of Cassius and Florentinus in Bonn. However, there is no evidence to suggest that the practice was diagnostically Christian, and is merely one of many late Roman burial practices which were deemed acceptable for a Christians to use.

Martyria and cemetery churches

The issue of churches within cemeteries has been briefly touched on in chapter 3, however, this needs to be considered in more detail. One of the enduring models for the development of Roman Christian cemeteries in towns, and the wider development of urban space in the Late Roman to early medieval period in Western Europe has been based around the notion of the *martyrium* or *cella memoriae*. Originally small shrines built over the believed burial place of early Christian martyrs the terms became extended to refer to shrines or holy places over any important members of the Christian communities, such as bishops and holy men. These shrines became the focus for burials of those who wished to be laid to rest within the aura of holiness created by these special graves. They also acted as magnets for the creation of larger church complexes. In some cases they became the focus for a wholesale shift in urban life. In cases, such as Tours, the Late Roman town within its city walls declined and was replaced by a new settlement that grew up around the burial place of St Martin in the fifth and sixth centuries.

Based on patterns recognised elsewhere in the Roman Empire, this model has sometimes been transferred to Britain. However, it has not proved possible to recognise parallel developments of this type. Few churches have been found within Christian cemetery sites. The best example of such a church is the structure from Butt Road. Although it is sited by a large, almost certainly Christian, burial site it is clearly not a *martyrium*. It stands at the north-west edge of the cemetery, not at the heart of the site, as might be expected if it was the focus of the Christian cemetery. There were three possible graves within the east end of the structure. One was on a different alignment and pre-dated the construction of the building *c*.AD 330. This unusual grave had probably contained a substantial timber vault for a single burial. The precise date of this burial is unclear, but it is most likely to have been an outlier from the Period 1, phase 2 cemetery. After the construction of the church, the other two graves were dug nearby; one aligned precisely on the building and the other at right angles. None of the burials contained any remains, although a later pit cut through the end of one grave did contain, among many other objects, a human skull and a leg bone, both probably from a young to middle-aged woman. Despite this church being on a cemetery and containing a few burials, it clearly never became a focus for burials. It is not possible to be exact, but it seems that the church and the newly organised cemetery at Butt Road were roughly contemporary. They may have both been part of a concerted attempt to lay out a Christian cemetery. The placement of the church over the wooden vaulted grave may have had some significance, and it may have been believed to be a holy grave, but the grave and the church never became the focus of the cemetery in the same way similar graves in mainland Europe did. It is more likely that the church's primary purpose was as a funerary banqueting hall, despite its possible origin as a *martyria*.

Another potential church associated with burials is the church in the small cemetery at Icklingham. However, again this church does not appear to have acted as a particular focus for the burials. Although two graves (G.40 and G.13) lie close to the southern walls of the structure, most of the graves lie over 20m to the south-east or 10m to the west. As at Butt Road, the building and the cemetery were probably laid out at the same time, rather than undergoing a period of organic growth around the church structure itself.

Less clear is the evidence surrounding the possible grave of St Alban in the town of *Verulamium*. A shrine to the martyr was recorded here as early as the sixth century AD, when the monk Gildas refers to the site as the most important shrine in Britain. However, much of the evidence has been destroyed by the later medieval cathedral of St Alban's, which has been built over the area of the Roman cemetery. It is clear that Late Roman burials were found in the area, and that many of them were aligned west-east and contained no grave-goods. However, no sign of a Roman church has been found, and any postulated development of the cathedral from a Roman *martyrium* cannot be proved. It is not possible to verify that the site developed as an important Christian focus within the Roman period. A Christian community is recorded in the town in the fifth century in the *Life of St Germanus*. Whilst the precise historical details of Germanus' visit in the mid-fifth century are unclear, it is a clear indication of continued contact between *Verulamium* and Gaul, and an example of the possible route through which the notion of the creation of a cemetery shrine may have arrived in south-east England in the post-Roman period.

In general, churches in Roman Britain appear never to have attracted burials. No graves are associated with the church at Silchester. Although burials have been found in and around the early churches at St Paul-in-the-Bail, Lincoln and St Mary de Lode, Gloucester, these all date to the sub-Roman period or later. This may be partly because in the late Roman period it was traditional to bury outside the walls of towns, and the churches mentioned above were all within them. However, it does show that the draw of burial near churches, which became important in the early medieval period had yet to become strong enough in the Roman period to overcome these traditional taboos.

Overall, the slight evidence for Britain fails to show any clear examples of the graves of holy individuals becoming the focal centres for Christian cemeteries or wider communities in the fourth century. Although churches may have stood in cemeteries, it does not appear that there was a belief that burial *ad sanctos*, that is in or near a church or holy grave was of great importance in the Roman period in Britain. In this respect, Christians in Roman Britain were not unlike those elsewhere in the Western Empire, where *martyria* did not develop as important shrines until the fifth century or late fourth century at the earliest.

Conclusions

It has been suggested that by the mid-fourth century, organized cemeteries in which most of the graves are aligned west-east and contain few, if any, grave-goods are likely to be Christian cemeteries. Whilst not everyone buried within such cemeteries may have been active Christians, they are likely to have been broadly favourable to Christianity, and not felt a need to overtly express their paganism in their burial rites.

7

CONCLUSIONS

In the last six chapters we have explored the historic and archaeological background to Christianity in Roman Britain. The approach taken was thematic, looking at the remains as they might have related to the main stages of the life of a typical Roman Christian. Many aspects of this life would have seemed familiar to a Christian from elsewhere in the Roman Empire. However, there were also many aspects of British Christianity which were unusual or distinct. The use of lead tanks for baptism or other ritual purposes was only found in Britain; nothing similar has been found in Gaul or elsewhere. Britain is also unusual in the number of precious metal hoards containing objects with Christian images. Similar hoards have certainly been found elsewhere in the Empire, but nowhere else is there such a concentration of discoveries. As well as these more obvious differences, there are more subtle variations. The use of peacocks on official belt buckle sets, for example, is unknown outside Britain. Despite the fact that these objects were manufactured to represent wider Imperial authority, they developed a distinctly British symbolic repertoire. Moving from these small personal artefacts to the largest aspect of Christian belief, church buildings, Britain's unusual nature persists. Unlike late Roman churches found in Gaul and elsewhere, many British churches appear to have been built from wood and do not show the same level of architectural elaboration. However, we need not to leap to any conclusions that the fourth-century church in Britain was somehow deviating from a wider imperial norm. By the beginning of the fifth century, Christendom covered a larger area than the Roman Empire, having expanded well into the Sassanian kingdom of Persia, into the Caucasus and south into Ethiopia. The religion that had been nourished by Constantine's fortuitous decision to convert had spilled beyond the territorial control of the imperial throne. It would have been more surprising if these Christian communities had shown any major uniformity. The distinctness of the British church is just what might be expected.

Any discussion of Christianity in Roman Britain inevitably has to confront the question of how widely spread the Church was by the end of the fourth century, or, as the question is more usually couched, was it a 'success' or a 'failure'? The normal approach to answering this query is to roughly quantify the archaeological evidence from the province and then cast around elsewhere in the Empire for comparisons against which such conclusions can be made. Whilst a great deal of effort is spent on assessing the extent to which particular objects or sites exhibit 'Christian' traits, less time is spent on considering the social context in which religious belief is expressed. Inevitably spectacular objects or finds, such as the Water Newton treasure or the Lullingstone wall paintings will score highly on any attempt to measure Christianity. However, to what extent are these discoveries more significant for quantifying Christianity than, for example, a crudely carved *chi-rho* on the base of a pot? Does the apparent cost of an object or wealth of the person or persons who commissioned it reflect the religious fervour which motivated its use, or like the parable of the Widow's mite, do the simple graffiti show a greater, more heartfelt attempt to express belief than the expensive wall paintings which could have been the passing whim of a late Roman aristocrat?

The situation becomes even thornier when we try and explore the influence of a religion. Late Roman Britain was not a democracy; the social influence of a particular ideology was not a simple function of the number of its believers, but was instead intimately tied up with issues of power. A religion may have relatively few followers, but due to their social position its influence may have spread far. We have seen how Christian symbols appeared in a range of official contexts, from belt sets to seals and coinage. Even if an individual does not follow a religion they may acknowledge its special position if it is seen to be intimately connected with secular sources of power.

These questions show the difficulty in trying to quantify the success or failure of Roman Christianity. The archaeological evidence is not a direct reflection of some notional 'level' of belief, but the product of the way in which people expressed their belief, which in turn was inevitably influenced by comparative levels of wealth, amongst many other social factors. The complex nature of this evidence means that maps showing the geographical distribution of objects and sites of possible Christian nature can only go so far in exploring the nature of the religion in Britain. In the same way that some of the unusual elements of Christianity in Roman Britain are just part of the wider variation in religious practice in the Empire, we need to be alive to the internal variations within the archaeology of Christianity in Britain. It is important then to relate these variable expressions of belief to differences in the social fabric of the country. Some of these modes of religious belief may have a geographical element and hence be indicated on maps, but others may be related to differences in status and class and thus not recognisable spatially. Despite the Church's constant vigilance against heresy, internal disagreement and sectarian tendencies, the congregations will have developed their own particular styles of worship and belief. It is by looking at these different styles of Christianity that we might get a better understanding of how the religion functioned in fourth-century Britain. Rather than creating an overarching model for the Church as a whole in the country, I want instead to see Christianity in Britain as being practised by a range of separate but related communities of belief, whose particular brands of worship may have followed differing trajectories as they moved into the fifth century.

Religion and towns

Across most of the Roman Empire, Christianity was initially an urban phenomenon. Communities sprung up amidst the great trading cities of the Eastern Mediterranean and followed the trade routes north and west. The ecclesiastical administration of the Church was centred on the bishops, who were usually urban. Although in some areas, such as North Africa, some of the larger rural estates, such as the one owned by Melania the Younger, could have their own bishops, these large farming centres were almost proto-urban in nature themselves. The textual evidence we have from Britain suggests that the same pattern was followed. The list of bishops from the Council of Arles suggests that a metropolitan bishop was based in each of the provincial capitals of the diocese. It is highly unlikely that these were the only bishops in Britain, particularly in the south and east, and there was presumably a network of subsidiary bishoprics, based on the existing administrative structure of *civitates*. However, although the towns of Roman Britain may have been the controlling nodes it is questionable how far Christianity in Britain was ever a truly urban phenomenon.

The first Roman towns were based on pre-existing Mediterranean urban traditions, with large quantities of public buildings and a strong belief in public benefaction. However, Gaul and Britain had no pre-existing tradition of urbanism before the Roman conquest, and the Romans imposed urban networks on these provinces. The extent to which urban life ever successfully took root in Britain is a heavily debated subject. Some early towns appear to have been successful, particularly those associated with the army or administration such as London, Chester and York. A number of *colonia*, inhabited by retired army veterans, such as Colchester and Lincoln also appear to have been successful. Notably, these towns were strongly influenced by communities from outside Britain who may have already been inculcated with the idea of town life. However, by the third century it was clear that whilst many towns continued to thrive, others were showing increasing evidence of difficulties.

They seem to have failed to develop as economic centres and instead survived primarily as administrative enclaves. Consequently, there appears to have been a decline in the level of construction of new public buildings, and those which had already been built often changed their use. They did, though, seem to continue as population centres, and contained large town houses. This slight decline in urbanism only appears to have applied to the larger Roman planned towns, there was a large number of smaller towns which appear to have developed organically, and these seem to have continued to act as centres for production and exchange well into the fourth century.

In Gaul, Britain's closest neighbour, the larger towns appear to have undergone a slow metamorphosis. Frequently, there appears to have been a period of shrinkage and retrenchment, leaving a smaller defended *enceinte*, which may have housed the administrative facilities of the *civitas*, including the bishop. These changes were traditionally related to the affects of the barbarian invasions of the 260s and 270s. However, there is increasing evidence to show that there was often still occupation outside the walled area, and that this process took place over a long period. In many ways in Britain the changes in urbanism differed from those in Gaul, where the change from early to late Roman towns was more pronounced. In particular they appear to have undergone a major decline in population, and the smaller towns also decline significantly in comparison with British examples.

However, despite the apparent greater urban transformations of Gaul, it was in the towns that the Gallic church appears to have found its roots. Almost all the evidence for stone churches and the structures associated with ecclesiastical complexes dates to the fifth century. The earlier fourth-century churches were smaller in size and less evidence survives for them. In this respect the Romano-British urban churches are very similar to those in Gaul, the real differences between the two areas did not really develop until the fifth century; this divergence is likely to have had as much to do with the differing nature of early medieval urbanism as the relative success or failure of the Church.

The possible Romano-British churches from cities appear to have varied in size. Those from Lincoln, Silchester and Colchester were fairly small, suggesting a relatively small congregation. However, the possible Christian basilica from London would have been more substantial. Ironically, the city of London underwent the most significant decline in size in the later Roman period, as the long-distance trade on which its wealth was based shrank. However, it continued to be the most important administrative centre in Britain, and if the basilica was indeed a church, then its size may reflect this administrative importance. Whilst the other urban churches are likely to have been funded by the local community, the London church could well have been an imperial foundation, hence its scale. However, the small size of the other churches need not automatically indicate a poor congregation. As we have already seen, there was a decline in public building in British towns, though this went hand in hand with a increased investment in large rural villas, some almost palatial in scale. It is this decision by the local elites not to invest in urban building projects which may explain the lack of major urban churches in Roman Britain. Given the relative lack of income for the bishops they may well have lived in typical Roman urban houses, rather than purpose-built complexes adjacent to their churches, making them harder to spot archaeologically.

But if there is little evidence for substantial church buildings within Romano-British towns, the evidence from cemeteries is different. If, as has been argued in this book, the simple 'managed' cemeteries with west-east aligned grave-goods were predominantly Christian then it appears that large numbers of Romano-British towns had Christian communities burying their dead in the local cemeteries. They appear to have been particularly associated with the small towns, such as Alcester, Alchester, Ashton and Great Casterton, rather than the larger *civitas* capitals, although some are associated with these bigger towns, such as the Batchwood cemetery at St Albans, Poundbury and Butt Road. These cemeteries are notable for the lack of expressions of wealth, although the exception is the Poundbury cemetery, with its decorated mausolea.

Other less spectacular fragments of Christianity from urban contexts in town include several vessels with *chi-rho* symbols carved as graffiti on their bases. Amongst these finds are pieces of a grey ware storage jar from Colchester with a *chi-rho* on the rim, a sherd from a black ware cooking jar from Exeter with the sign on the shoulder and a colour-coated bowl from Kelvedon with religious graffiti on the base. Such marks were not limited to pottery vessels and a small *chi-rho* was found scratched onto the base of a pewter bowl from Caerwent. The reasons behind the carving of these small symbols are unclear, though they do not seem to be used in an official context. They could be simple good-luck or protective charms, although they clearly show a familiarity with Christian symbolism.

The most striking aspect of Christianity in large Romano-British cities is its relatively low level. The churches are mainly small and unimpressive and the other evidence such as the graffiti is important, but does not indicate a large investment in religious objects. Although there is evidence for Christian cemeteries these are far more common from small towns and large rural settlements. Unlike their Gaulish counterparts the important Roman cities of Britain appear not to have become important centres of Christianity. Although some cities, such as the provincial capitals, may have had bishops and associated episcopal complexes the towns appear to have never developed large urban congregations. However, this does not mean that the Church in Britain was necessarily stunted. To better understand the spread of Christianity we need to turn to the wider rural landscape of Britain, with its small market towns and large rural centres. It is here that we can get a better understanding of the way in which Christianity integrated with late Roman society.

Eastern England

If Christianity appears to have failed to take root in the larger towns it seems to have been more successful in some rural areas, particularly East Anglia and the East Midlands. It is this area that has provided the evidence for most lead tanks and Christian hoards. However, as we saw in earlier chapters this may be because a pre-existing tradition of placing votive objects in ritual pits or watery locations was strongest in this region. This would mean that the apparent focus of Christian activity here might have been caused by local traditions of religious worship which left a distinctive archaeological footprint. However, these ritually deposited objects, as well as the evidence from cemeteries and possible churches means that we can begin to see quite dense landscapes of Christian activity. The area around Icklingham with its dense pattern of Christian and pagan objects has already been explored in detail, but other areas of this region also show relatively dense levels of Christian remains.

The large rural settlement of Ashton lies close to the River Nene on the road leading to Water Newton. It is a typical example of a Roman undefended small town with properties strung out along the main road and smaller side roads providing access to the other buildings. To the north of the main road a series of large ditched enclosures were built. The town contains an excellent example of a 'managed' cemetery, which stood to the south-west of the main built-up area. This burial site contrasted with the expected cluster of burials in varied positions in the rear of the enclosures built along the main road. Nearby, at the south-west angle of a crossroads stood a large structure with a courtyard. The presence of five furnaces and large quantities of iron slag suggested that this was probably a blacksmith's workshop. In the northern part of the courtyard was a deep well. A complete lead tank with the *chi-rho* monogram came from this well, along with fragments of a second tank. This conjunction of two Christian lead tanks and a Christian cemetery is a clear indicator of the level of the support of the church in this region.

If we zoom out from the settlement of Ashton we can see that it is just one of many sites which have produced evidence for Christianity. Ten miles to the north was the small town of Great Chesterton, also sitting on the River Nene. Just outside the town, the famous Water Newton treasure was discovered. To the west, at Orton Longueville a strap-end showing a Christian peacock symbol was found. Another was found ten miles to the south of Ashton at Thrapston, not far from the Roman small town at Titchmarsh. A further cluster of Christian belt equipment was found further south, with two peacock decorated strap-ends from Milton Keynes (Bucks.) and one bearing a *chi-rho* from Sandy (Beds.). A peacock-decorated belt buckle was also found around 30 miles to the west at the small town of *Tripontium* (Cave's End Farm, Warks.). Probable Christian cemeteries were found at a number of small towns in the area including one from the large ironworking settlement at Laxton (Northants) and others at Bletsoe (Beds.) and Great Casterton (Rutland).

The most important aspects of Roman Christianity in the east of England are the contrasts between the dense patterns of lead tanks, cemeteries and hoards and the almost complete lack of church structures. The church at Icklingham is very small, and sites such as Ivy Chimneys, Witham, have produced no convincing evidence of a significant church building despite the presence of a font. However, the discovery of extremely wealthy hoards, such as that from Water Newton, show that the Christian congregations in this area were not poor. The lack of investment in church buildings appears not to have been caused by poverty. Instead it seems to be part of a wider difference between western and eastern England. The east of England has a wider lack of extensive investment in architecturally elaborate buildings. Unlike the south-west there appears not to have been a late Roman flowering of villa construction, despite the continued success of the small Roman towns, such as Water Newton and Ashton. The lack of church building is an indicator of a wider difference in the way in which wealth was deployed in eastern England. Rather than spending surplus on building pagan temples, Christian churches or secular buildings such as villas, excess wealth seems to have been spent on more portable indicators of wealth, such as silver and gold plate, jewellery and other smaller objects.

Western England

This emphasis on portable religious objects at the expense of investment in buildings contrasts with the pattern in south-western Britain. In the fourth century a series of splendid and architecturally elaborate villas were built in this region, and there was an apparent flowering of 'villa life'. These large villas were found particularly in the areas surrounding the provincial capital of Cirencester (*Corinium*) and the *civitas* capital Dorchester. The fourth century also saw an increase in the number of rural temples being built, whilst at the same time there was a decrease in the number of urban temples. A mid fourth-century peak is found for both rural temples and villas. Although most pronounced in the south-west this broad pattern is found across much of southern and central England, although not as we have seen the East Midlands and East Anglia.

This expression of religious belief and social status through architectural elaboration extends to Christianity. It is in these areas that we have best built evidence for the religion. To the east are the wall paintings of Lullingstone. Although outside the main area of fourth-century building it was one of a cluster of high-status villas in the north of Kent. In the south-west we have already seen the clearly Christian mosaics at Frampton and Hinton St Mary.

Perhaps the greater interest in using buildings to express social identity explains why the cemetery at Poundbury contained so many mausolea.

Although bricks, mortar and tesserae appear to have been the most obvious ways of demonstrating power they were not the only ones. There is no clear evidence for a large-scale tradition of votive hoarding and deposition, though individual Christian objects are known. For example, silver rings with *chi-rho* symbols are known from a number of villa sites. A lead tank was also found in the possible small town at Bourton-on-the-Water. As in eastern Britain there is also ample evidence for Christian burial. As well as the cemeteries at Poundbury, Dorset, and Ilchester there are simple managed cemeteries outside small towns, such as Dorchester-on-Thames (Oxon.) and Tiddington (Warks.).

Christianity and the army

So far the two main patterns of Christian worship discussed have been defined geographically, with a broad east-west divide. However, many of the major divisions in Romano-British society were based as much on social groups as regional variations. Perhaps the best example of a regionally diffuse social group is the army. Although the *limitatenses* were by definition found mainly on the borders of the diocese, the *comitatenses* would have been stationed all over Roman Britain.

The relationship between the Roman army and Christianity in Britain is one that recent scholarship has changed our understanding of most radically. When Jocelyn Toynbee wrote her overview of Christianity in Roman Britain in 1953 she noted that 'The picture painted by archaeology is . . . almost wholly civilian in its context'. In a more recent exploration of the topic G.R. Watson added little. Much of the evidence for the Roman army's interest in the religion appeared to have been primarily negative, relating to apparent destruction of pagan religious sites in military areas, such as the destruction of the mithraeum at Carrawburgh (Northumberland). However, archaeological remains of Christianity are being increasingly recognised.

The first class of evidence we have for military Christianity is the remains of churches from forts. In chapter 3 we saw that probable or possible churches have been found at Richborough (Kent), South Shields (Tyne and Wear), Housesteads (Northumberland), Chesterholm/*Vindolanda* (Northumberland) and Birdoswald (Northumberland). These appear to have been built in either the main principia or headquarters area of the fort or the north-west corner. The range of building materials appears to have been varied depending on locality. The Richborough church was probably built of timber and supported on post-pads, but in the north where there was easier access to stone the buildings appear to have mainly been of stone. There is difficulty in providing precise dates for these buildings, although they are likely to have been later fourth-century in date, rather than earlier. The two churches built on the site of the headquarters buildings, South Shields and Chesterholm are very late, possibly even early fifth century. Their position suggests that they may be replacing earlier pagan regimental shrines. It is noticeable that at Richborough and possibly Housesteads there are the remains of possible fonts.

The second major class of evidence for Christianity in the military areas of Britain are gravestones. The recognition of a distinct group of late Roman memorial stones with likely Christian epitaphs is important, as they gives us a direct insight into the composition of the congregations. Tombstones from Cawfields and Templeborough record the burial of soldiers from outside Britain: Dagvalda from Pannonia (present day Serbia) and Crotus son of Vindex from Gaul. These are the only inscriptions which explicitly record members of the army. However, it is possible that the men recorded on tombstones from Brougham and Maryport were also soldiers. Crucially, women and children also appear on some of these stones, both as commemorator and commemorated. Finally, as well as the two tombs of foreigners mentioned above there are at least two on which the name is clearly of native British origin: Tancorix, recorded on a stone from Old Carlisle and Rianorix on one from Maryport. These burial monument gives us a good cross-section of the Christian communities associated with these military churches. They included soldiers and civilians, women and children, natives and foreigners. This implies that the churches associated with forts were serving the wider community and were not limited to the military, although it is possible that there are churches still to be found in the vicinity, frequently associated with military sites. The presence of fonts also implies that these churches were at the centre of an active congregation in which people were undergoing instruction and religious education. The military churches were clearly more than simple regimental chapels, but had responsibilities beyond the walls of the forts.

So far most of this evidence has focused on evidence from the military borders of Britain, and is primarily related to the religious affiliations of the *limitatenses*. This is partly because it is easier to recognise distinct military communities along the well-defended frontiers. The *comitatenses* were billeted amongst civilians in towns in the civilian zones. This makes it harder to recognise the military communities against the background noise of civilian occupation. One of the few groups of objects that may well be a good indicator of a military presence in civilian areas are the distinct group of belt buckles discussed in chapter 5. Even these may have also been used by members of the imperial civil service. The thirteen belt buckles or strap-ends with Christian symbols from Britain are found spread widely across the civilian area of Roman Britain, straddling the broad divide in Christian practice noted between the east and west. They come from a range of sites, small towns, such as *Tripontium*, Harlow and Kenchester to villas such as Wortley (Glos.) and Beadlam (North Yorks.) and other rural settlements such as Wavendon Gate (Bucks.) and Rushall Down

(Wilts.). It is noticeable though that none of these objects come from *civitas* capitals or other large towns. If these buckles and strap-ends were indeed worn by the mobile field army it suggests that they were stationed out in small towns and rural sites rather than in large urban centres.

Allowing for the difficulties in clearly distinguishing military communities in civilian areas it does appear that Christianity was important within the Roman army in Britain. No pagan religious imagery appears on belt buckles and strap-ends and the stone gravestones of northern Britain appear to be primarily Christian. The presence of a series of churches in important locations within Roman forts is also highly significant. Other Christian objects from military sites include rings bearing *chi-rho* monograms found at Brancaster (Suffolk) and Brough-under-Stainmore (Cumbria). There are also two hoards with possible military connections; the group of silver objects found in the Tyne near Corbridge, and the hoard of objects from Traprain Law. These may both also indicate wealthy Christian communities in the north of Britain. It is also important to remember that if St Patrick is to be located in the north of Britain, possible from a vicus along Hadrian's Wall, then this is further evidence for Christianity in the military zone.

It is increasingly being recognised that in the late Roman period the close rela-tionship between the Roman army units along the northern frontiers and the nearby civilian settlements led to the development of a distinct Romano–British military culture. It is not possible to separate the religion of soldiers from their wives, children and associates. The evidence from the gravestones suggests both military and civilians were members of these northern Christian communities.

Relationships between Christians and pagans

Even the most optimistic advocate of the success of Christianity in Roman Britain would not deny that the majority of the population remained pagan. The only debate is how great this majority was. Undoubtedly there would have been immense regional variation. Although Christianity was not the dominant religion in purely numerical terms, its position as the ideological arm of the Empire allowed it to 'punch above its weight'. The relationship between paganism and Christianity must have varied. We know from the lead tablet from Bath that at least one person saw religious life in Britain as divided between Christians and others, he called 'gentiles'. It has often been suggested that the relationship between the two camps was sometimes tense, and there may have been cases when Christians actively destroyed pagan religious sites in acts of religiously motivated violence. The mithraea at London and Carrawburgh (Northumberland) were both apparently victims of vicious attempts to damage them. The statues in Carrawburgh were deliberately broken, but the altars remained in position. Although the Walbrook

Mithraeum was attacked in the early fourth century, pagan worship soon resumed there. In other cases pagan altars or tombstones were reused for secular purposes, such as road repair in Corbridge or as linings for burials at Ancaster and York. The treatment of pagan sculpture was not always so functional; three altars and five sculptures were tipped into a well in Lower Slaughter (Glos.). The problems with these apparent outbursts of anti-pagan violence include the difficulty in dating them, and deducing the motivation. For example, it is not clear whether the destruction of Wallbrook Mithraeum pre- or post-dated the freedom of the Church. Even if it did post-date 313 it is uncertain whether Christian communities at this early date would have been strong enough to attack a pagan religious site, particularly one with such close links to the military. The question of motivation applies to the destruction of the Carrawburgh temple; if it was a victim of Christian intolerance then why did the altars remain standing? In the case of the more functional reuse of sculpture there is no need to subscribe to an anti-pagan justification. The reuse of architectural stone or *spolia* for such practical purposes was widespread in the late Roman period, and need have no religious motivation. There were certainly outbursts of anti-pagan violence in Gaul, and Sulpicius Severus' *Life of St Martin* recorded this militant bishop's destruction of several pagan religious sites. However, the evidence that such campaigns were carried out in Britain is absent. Although there may have been occasional outbursts of intra-community violence, there seems to have been no orchestrated campaign against paganism.

The evidence for Christianity from Roman Britain is not vast, but it is respectable when compared with evidence for other specific cults. Considering that there were less than one hundred years between the freedom of the Church and the end of Roman rule in Britain the evidence is widespread and significant. There are certainly aspects of Christianity in which Britain appears to be very poorly provided, specifically church buildings. However, as we have seen there are very distinct methodological problems with distinguishing churches from secular buildings. Comparisons with the level of church building in Britain and the Continent often fails to compare like with like. There are definitely few certain fourth-century churches in Britain, but the same is true for much of Gaul, particularly the northern areas. Even many of the fourth-century Gaulish churches have only been recognised on the basis of continuity of ecclesiastical use on the site allowing the function of the site to be projected back into the fourth century. The perceived differences between Britain and Gaul are related more to the structure of fifth- and sixth-century Christianity than the situation in the fourth century. The unique aspects of Christianity in Britain such as the use of lead tanks and the plate hoards should be seen not as the idiosyncratic developments of an isolated and unorthodox church, but as typical of the range of religious practices in the Christian world in the fourth and fifth centuries. The historical evidence certainly shows that in these centuries Britain was in frequent contact with important ecclesiastical figures in Gaul and elsewhere. It should come as no surprise to find that in the late fourth century Romano-British Christians were recorded by Jerome as pilgrims in the Holy Land.

The archaeological evidence from Britain shows that Christianity appears to have been accepted across much of the country, and was known from the northern borders on Hadrian's Wall to Richborough, the gateway to the Continent. Considering its wide distribution it is no surprise that there are variations in the way in which it was practised across the diocese. The biggest contrast is between the west and east of lowland Britain. In the east Christian belief appears to have incorporated the practice of votive deposition already common in pagan traditions in the area. In the west a greater emphasis appears to have been placed on building religious structures, both temples and Christian sites. These variations in Christian practice were clearly intimately related to the pre-existing nature of paganism in each region. Archaeology is also beginning to show the importance of Christianity in the army in Roman Britain. Along the northern border the Church seems to have had a particularly important role in both military and civilian life.

One of the most important differences between Britain and the rest of the Empire was the relationship between Christianity and towns. Across most of the Empire the Church was pre-eminently an urban phenomenon, with the most powerful communities being centred in the biggest towns. However, in *Britannia*, although the church appeared in towns it seems never to have bloomed. Churches are known, but they seem to be small. Instead it is in the countryside and the small towns in particular that Christianity appears to have been strongest. In the East Midlands in particular, many small towns have produced evidence of Christian communities, either in the form of cemeteries, baptismal tanks or other objects. Unlike Gaul these low-level urban centres continued to thrive in the fourth century, and it is in these thriving centres that the church appears to have really taken root, rather than the increasingly stale major towns. If it is the small towns and the countryside that were the homes for late Roman Britain's social vitality, then it is not surprising that these should be the prime breeding grounds of the Church rather than the larger towns. Although the impact of Anglo-Saxon political take-over wiped clean much of the slate in eastern England, the evidence from western Britain suggests that it was these smaller towns that continued to form the basis of the early medieval episcopal structure.

In a series of articles, Steven Basset has located a number of pre-Saxon dioceses in the West Midlands, which were often foci for later Saxon dioceses or minster churches. These centres were usually late Roman small towns. He suggests that St Helen's, Worcester, was a British foundation, only later being eclipsed by the cathedral. He tentatively outlines the former parish of St Helen's, relating it to a discrete territory around the city, which probably had its origins in the Roman period. Elsewhere he explores the relationship between Lichfield and the Roman town at Wall (*Letocetum*). He suggests that the church of St Michael's at Lichfield is a British foundation, and that it was related to a putative earlier foundation at *Letocetum*, which can probably be identified with *Caer Lwytgoed* raided by Morfael, King of Powys, as recorded in the poem *Marwnad Cynddylan*, possibly in the seventh century. The poem seems to explicitly indicate that *Caer Lwytgoed* was the seat of a bishop:

> Magnificent was the combat, great the booty,
> Before Caer Lwytgoed Morfael took
> Fifteen hundred cattle and five herds of [?] swine
> Eighty stallions with their accompanying harness
> Not a single bishop in four corners
> Nor book-holding monks were afforded protection
> *Marwnad Cynddylan*

(trans. Kirby 1977, 37)

He also suggests, with less certainty, that Wroxeter, with its minster church at St Andrew's and Gloucester, with the early church of St Mary de Lode were also centres of British pre-Saxon ecclesiastical territories, probably based on even earlier Roman territories.

It is the integration of Christianity into the rural world that allowed the Church to weather the disruptive effects of the warfare and political conflict of the fifth century. Although life in towns changed radically in this period, this did not trouble the Church, which was already developing a semi-rural rather than semi-urban infrastructure. It was the flexibility that this provided which allowed the Christian Church to re-emerge as the centrally important institution in the early medieval period. It is noticeable that early medieval writers such as Gildas firmly believed that Christianity was a Roman introduction, and there are no traditions of a renewed period of missionary activity or proselytising in the early fifth century. Many commentators have seen the failure of the Church in Romano-British towns as a failure of the Church elsewhere. Frend has suggested that the Church failed to develop in Britain, as there were no figures of the stature of Martin of Tours who were willingly to actively take the Church to the pagan rural areas surrounding the urban bastions of the faith. However, the nature of late Gaulish society was different to that in Britain. If Britain had no figure like St Martin, perhaps is because it did not need one.

The important role of the church in the transition into the post-Roman period also occurred in the north. The Church had made great progress amongst communities along the northern border, both military and civilian, if such a distinction can still be made at this period. Archaeological evidence is increasingly showing that many forts continued to be occupied into the fifth century. Long hall-type buildings have been excavated at Birdoswald, and possible early medieval refortifications are known from other forts, such as South Shields. Christianity appears to have also continued to be important for many of these early medieval communities. A small portable altar of fifth- or sixth-century date has been found at Chesterholm. A rare early Christian gravestone has also been found nearby. It is the strength of Christianity in these areas in the fifth century which may explain the rapid expansion of the Church over the old political borders, and its rapid success in Dumfries and Galloway, particularly around the important monastic site of Whithorn. It is from these northern strongholds that the church may also have also have rapidly reached much of lowland Scotland.

By the end of the Late Roman period the Church was firmly established in Roman Britain and ready to be taken beyond the traditional edges of Empire. Loyalty to the Church was rapidly replacing loyalty to the Empire. By participating in the spread of Christendom it was possible to participate vicariously in the prestige and power of the Empire, without surrendering political power. The story of the rise and spread of the early medieval Church in Britain is not one for this book, but it would never have been possible without the initial success of the Romano-British Church in the fourth century.

SELECT BIBLIOGRAPHY

General works

Anyone wishing to pursue further reading on Christianity in Roman Britain should turn to Charles Thomas' *Christianity in Roman Britain to AD 500* (1981, London). This lays out the main historical framework and gives effective overviews of most categories of the archaeological evidence. The best exposition of the evidence of the portable objects is Frances Mawer's *Evidence for Christianity in Roman Britain: The Small Finds* (1995, British Archaeological Reports 243, Oxford). Two other general studies from the 1990s are *Christians and Pagans in Roman Britain* (1991, London) and *Religion in Late Roman Britain: Forces of Change* (1998, London) both by Dorothy Watts. A little dated, but containing some valuable papers is *Christianity in Britain, 300-700* (1968, Leicester) edited by M.W. Barley and R.P.C. Hanson.

1 Looking at Roman Britain

Collingwood, R. 1923. *Roman Britain,* Oxford

Cookson, N. 1987. 'The Christian church in Roman Britain: a synthesis of archaeology' World Archaeology, 18, 426–33

Dark, K.R. 1994. *Civitas to Kingdom: British Political Continuity 300-800,* (Leicester)

Dark, K.R. 2000. *Britain and the End of the Roman Empire,* (Stroud)

Esmonde Cleary, S. 1989. *The Ending of Roman Britain,* (London)

Faulkner, N., 2000. *Decline and Fall of Roman Britain,* (Stroud)

Frend, W.H.C. 1955. 'Religion in Roman Britain in the Fourth Century' *Journal of British Archaeological Association,* (3rd Series) 18, 1–18

Frend, W.H.C. 'The Christianisation of Roman Britain' in Barley, M.W. & Hanson, R.P.C. (eds) *Christianity in Roman Britain 300-700,* (Leicester), 37–50 (1968)

Frend, W.H.C. 1979. '*Ecclesia Britannica*: prelude or dead end' *Journal of Ecclesiastical History,* 30, 129–44

Frend, W.H.C. 1992. 'Pagans, Christians and the "Barbarian Conspiracy" of AD367 in Roman Britain' *Britannia* 23, 121–32

Frend, W.H.C. 1996. *The Archaeology of Early Christianity: A History,* (London)

Frere, S.S. 1987 *Britannia: A History of Roman Britain,* (London)

Gibbon, E. *Decline and Fall of the Roman Empire,*

Haverfield, F. 1896. 'Early History of Christianity in Britain' *English Historical Review* 11

Haverfield, F. 1905. *The Romanization of Britain,* (London)

Henig, M. 1984. *Religion in Roman Britain,* (London)

Henig, M. 1995. *The Art of Roman Britain,* (London)

Higham, N.J. 1992. *Rome, Britain and the Anglo-Saxons,* (London)

Jones, M. *The End of Roman Britain,* (London)

Mawer, F. 1995. *Evidence for Christianity in Roman Britain: The Small Finds,* (Oxford)

Millett, M. 1990. *The Romanisation of Britain: An Essay in Archaeological Interpretation,* (Cambridge)

Morris, J.R. 1965. 'Pelagian Literature' *Journal of Theological Studies,* 16, 26–60

Myres, J.N.L. 1960. 'Pelagius and the end of Roman Britain' *Journal of Roman Studies,* 50, 21–36

Myres, J.N.L. 1902. *The English Settlements,* (Oxford)

Perring, D. 2002. *The Roman House in Britain,* (London)

Rahtz, P. 1982. 'Celtic Society in Somerset AD400–700 '*Bulletin of the Board of Celtic Studies,* 30, 176–200

Thomas, C. 1971. *The Early Christian Archaeology of North Britain,* (Edinburgh)

Thomas, C. 1981. *Christianity in Roman Britain to AD500,* (London)

Toynbee, J. 1953. 'Christianity in Roman Britain' *Journal of the British Archaeological Association,* 16, 1–24

Williams, H. 1912 *Christianity in Early Britain,* (Oxford)

Objects and sites

Binchester	Hoopell, R.E. 1879. *Vinovia: The Buried Roman City at Binchester,* (Bishop Auckland)
Colchester	Crummy, N. Crummy, P. & Crossan, C. 1993. *Colchester Archaeological Report 9: Excavations of Roman and Later Cemeteries, churches and monastic sites in Colchester, 1971-88,* (Colchester)
Icklingham	West, S.E. and Plouviez, J. 1976. 'The Roman Site at Icklingham' *East Anglian Archaeology,* 63-125
Hinton St Mary	Eriksen, R.T. 1982. 'Syncretistic symbolism and the Christian Roman mosaic at Hinton St Mary: a closer reading' Proceedings of the Dorset natural History and Archaeological Society, 102, 43-8 Painter, K.S. 1967. 'The Roman Site at Hinton St Mary, Dorset' *British Museum Quarterly,* 32 (1-2), 15-31

	Toynbee, J.M.C. 1964. 'The Christian Roman Mosaic, Hinton St Mary, Dorset' Proceedings of the Dorset Archaeological Society 85, 116-21
Long Wittenham	Henig, M and Booth, P. 2001. *Roman Oxfordshire,* (Stroud)
Lullingstone	Meates, G.W. 1979. *The Roman Villa at Lullingstone: Vol.1 The Site,* (Maidstone) Meates, G.W. et al. 1987. *The Roman Villa at Lullingstone, Vol.2 The Wall Paintings and Finds,* (Maidstone)
Mildenhall	Painter, K.S. 1977. *The Mildenhall treasure: Roman Silver from East Anglia,* (London)
Risley	Johns, C. 1981. 'The Risley Park Lanx: A Lost Antiquity from Roman Britain' *Antiquaries Journal,* 61, 53-72; Johns, C. & Painter, K. *1991. 'The Risley Park Lanx Rediscovered',* Minerva 2 (6), 6-13
Silchester	Ford, S.D. 1994 'The Silchester Church: A Dimensional Analysis and a New Reconstruction', 25, 119-26 Frere, S.S. 1975. 'The Silchester Church: The Excavations by Sir Ian Richmond in 1961' *Archaeologia,* 105, 277-302 King, A. 1983. 'The Silchester Church Reconsidered' *Oxford Journal of Archaeology,* 2, 225-37
Traprain Law	Curle. A.O. 1923. *The Treasure of Traprain Law,* (Glasgow)
Water Newton	Frend, W.H.C. 1984-5. 'Syrian parallels to the Water Newton treasure?' *Jahrbuch für Antike und Christentum,* 27-8, 146-50 Painter, K.S. 1977. *The Water Newton Early Christian Silver* (London) Painter, K.S. 1999. 'The Water Newton Silver: Votive or Liturgical?' *Journal of the British Archaeological Association,* 152, 1-23
Historical texts	
Bede	*Ecclesiastical History of the English People* edited and translated Sherley-Price, L (1990, London)
Geoffrey of Monmouth	*The History of the Kings of Britain,* translated L. Thorpe (1982, London)
Gildas	*De Excidio The Ruin of Britain,* edited and translated M. Winterbottom (1978, Chichester)

Nennius   *Historia Brittonum British History and The Welsh Annals*
                        edited and translated J. Morris (1980, Chichester)
Polydore Vergil   *Historia Anglica,* (1972, London)
Verstegan, John   *A Restitution of decayed Intelligence in Antiquities,*
                        (1976, Ilkley)
William   *The History of the English Kings,* edited and translated
of Malmesbury   R.A.B. Mynors (1998, Oxford)

2 Historical background

Cameron, A. *The Later Roman Empire AD284-403,* (Cambridge)

Esmonde Cleary, S. 1989. *The Ending of Roman Britain,* (London)

Henig, M. 2001. 'Religion and Art in St Alban's City ' in M. Henig (ed) *Alban and Saint Albans: Roman and Medieval Art, Architecture and Archaeology,* (Leeds), 1-13

Jones, A.H.M. 1948. *Constantine and the Conversion of Europe,* (London)

Jones, A.H.M. 1964. *The Later Roman Empire 284-602,* (London)

Jones and Galliou, P. 1994. *The Bretons,* (Oxford)

Knight, J. 2001. 'Britain's Other Martyrs: Julius, Aaron and Alban in Caerleon', in Henig (ed), 30-5

Sharpe, R. 2001. 'The Late Antique Passio of St Alban', in Henig, M. (ed.), 13-34

Salway, P. 1981. *Roman Britain,* (Oxford)

Objects and sites

Bath Tablet   Tomlin, R.S.O. 1988. 'The Curse Tablets' in B.
                        Cunliffe (ed.) *The Temple of Sulis Minverva at Bath.*
                        Vol II: The Finds from the Sacred Spring, (Oxford), 59-
                        277

Cirencester chi-rho   Atkinson, , D. 1951. 'The Origin and Date of the *Sator*
                        Word Square' *Journal of Ecclesiastical History,* 76, 21-31

Isle of Ely   Clarke, L.G.C. 1931. 'Roman Pewter Bowl from the
                        Isle of Ely' *Proceedings of the Cambridge Antiquarian*
                        Society, 31, 66-75

Manchester chi-rho   Green, M.J. 1976. *A Corpus of Religious Material from*
                        the Civillian Areas of Roman Britain, British
                        Archaeological Reports (British Series) 24,
                        (Oxford), 64

Risley Park   See references for Chapter 1

Shavington   Penney, S. and Shotter, D.C.A. 1996 'An Inscribed Salt
                        Pan from Shavington, Cheshire', *Britannia* 27, 360-5

Water Newton   See references for Chapter 1

Historical texts
British section of
Acta Concilii Arelatensis   Rivet, A.L.F. and Smith, C.C., 1979. *The Place-Names of Roman Britain,* (London), 49–102

Eusebius   *Life of Constantine,* translated and edited by A. Cameron and S. Hall (1999, Oxford)

Lactantius   *De Mortibus Persecutorum, (On the Deaths of the Persecutors),* translated and edited by Creed, J.L. (1984, Oxford)

Origen   *Selections from the Commentaries and Homilies of Origen,* translated by R.B. Tollington (1929, London)

Constantius of Lyon   *The Life of St. Germanus of Auxerre,* edited and trans lated by T. Noble and T. Head in *Soldiers of Christ: Saints' Lives from Late Antiquity and the Early Middle Ages,* (1994, Philadelphia), 75–106

Gerontius of Jerusalem   *The Life of Melania the Younger,* translated and edited by E. Clark (1984, New York)

Victricius of Rouen   *De Laude Sanctorum* Migne *Patrologia Latina,* 20, 443–58

Prosper of Aquitaine   *Chronicle,* Momsen, M.G.H. *Auctores Antiquissimi,* 9 *(Chronica Minora 1),* 464–85

On the Seven Offices
of the Church   Griffé, E.1966. *La Gaule Chrétienne à l'Époque Romaine Vol II,* (Paris-Toulouse), 312–22

Jerome   *On Illustrious Men,* edited and translated by T.Halton (1999, New York)

Sidonius Apollinaris   *Poems and Letters,* translated and edited W.B. Anderson (1965, Cambridge)

St Patrick   *Confessio,* St Patrick: His Writings and Muirchu's Life. Translated and edited A.B.E. Hood (1978, Chichester)

Zosimus   *New History,* edited and translated by R.T. Ridley (1982, Sidney)

3 The Church

Krautheimer, R. 1979. *Early Christian and Byzantine Architecture,* (Harmondsworth)
Dix, G. 2001. *The Shape of the Liturgy,* (London)

Objects and sites
Colchester   See references for Chapter 1
Brean Down   Ap Simon, A. 1964–5. 'The Roman Temple on Brean Down, Somerset' *Proceedings of the Speleological Society* 10 (3), 195–258

	Bell, M. et al. 1990. *Brean Down Excavations 1983-87,* (London)
Dura Europos	Baur, P.V.C. and Hopkins, C. 1934. *Christian Church at Dura Europos,* (Yale)
Hinton St Mary	See references in Chapter 1
Housesteads	Crow, J. 1995 *The English Heritage Book of Housesteads,* (London)
Icklingham	See references in Chapter 1
Lamyatt Beacon	Leech, R. 1986. 'The Excavation of a Romano-Celtic temple and a later cemetery on Lamyatt Beacon, Somerset' *Britannia,* 17, 259-328
Lincoln: St Paul	Jones, M.J. 1994. 'St Paul in the Bail, Lincoln: Britain in Europe?' in K. Painter (ed.) *'Churches Built in Ancient Times'. Recent Studies in Early Christian Archaeology,* (London), 325-47
Flaxengate	Colyer, C. and Jones, M.J. 1979. 'Excavations at Lincoln. Second Interim Report: Excavations in the Lower Town' *Antiquaries Journal,* 59, 50-91
London	Sankey, D., 1998. 'Cathedrals, granaries and urban vitality in late Roman London' in B. Watson (ed.) *Roman London: Recent Archaeological Work,* (1998, Portsmouth), 78-82
Lullingstone	See references in Chapter 1
Maiden Castle	Wheeler, R.E.M 1943. *Maiden Castle, Dorset* (London) Nettleton Shrubs Wedlake, W.J. 1982. *The Excavation of the Shrine of Apollo at Nettleton 1956- 71,* (London)
Richborough	Brown, P.D.C. 1971. 'The Church at Richborough, Kent' *Britannia,* 2, 225-31
Silchester	See references in Chapter 1
South Shields	Bidwell, P. and Speak, S. 1994. *Excavations at South Shields Roman Fort, vol.1,* (Newcastle Upon Tyne)
Uley	Woodward, A. and Leech, P. 1993. *The Uley Shrines: Excavation of a Ritual Complex on West Hill, Uley, Gloucestershire, 1977-9,* (London)
Verulamium	Biddle, M. and Kjølbye-Biddle, B. 2001. 'The Origins of St Alban Abbey: Romano-British Cemetery and Anglo-Saxon Monastery' in Henig, M. (ed), 45-78 Wheeler, R.E.M. and Wheeler, T.V., 1936. *Verulamium: A Belgic and Two Roman Cities,* (London)
Water Newton	See references in Chapter1

Witham   Turner, R. 1999. *Excavations of an Iron-Age Settlement and a Roman Religious Complex at Ivy Chimneys, Witham 1978-83*, East Anglian Archaeology 88

4   Becoming Christian

McKillop, S. 1982. 'A Romano-British baptismal liturgy' in Pearce, S. (ed.) *The early Church in Western Britain and Ireland*, British Archaeological Reports 102, (Oxford), 35-48

Perring, D. 2002. *The Roman House in Britain,* (London), 182

Objects and sites

Ashton   Guy, C.J. 1977. 'The lead tank from Ashton' *Durobrivae,* **5**, 6-9

Bourton   Donovan, H.E. 1934, 'Excavations of a Romano-British building at Bourton on the Water' *Transactions of the Bristol and Gloucester Archaeological Society,* **55**, 98-128

Chedworth   Goodburn, R. 1972. *The Roman Villa, Chedworth,* (London), Pl.11

Colchester   See reference in Chapter 1

Housesteads   See reference in Chapter 1, 95-6, fig.62

Icklingham   See reference in Chapter 1

Lead tanks   Guy, C.J., 1981. 'Roman Circular Lead Tanks in Britain' *Britannia,* **12**, 271-6

Pulborough   Curwen, E.C., 1943. 'Roman Lead Cistern from Pulborough, Sussex' *Antiquaries Journal,* **23**, 155-7

Richborough   See Brown in Chapter 3

Silchester   See Frere in Chapter 3

Walesby   Petch, D.F. 1961. 'A Roman lead tank, Walesby' *Lincolnshire Architectural. Archaeological Society Report,* **9**, 13-15

Witham   See reference in Chapter 3

5   Being Christain

Green, M. and Ferguson, J. 1987 'Constantine, sun-symbols and the labarum' *Durham University Journal,* 49, 9-17

Henig, M. 1984. *Religion in Roman Britain,* (London)

Manning, W.H., 1972. 'Ironwork Hoards in Iron Age and Roman Britain' *Britannia* **3**, 224–50

Peal, C.A. 1967 'Romano-British pewter plates and dishes' *Proceedings of the Cambridge Antiquarian Society,* **60**, 19-37

Perring, D. 2002. *The Roman House in Britain,* (London)

Petts, D. 2002. 'Votives in Late Roman Britain: Pagan or Christian?' in M. Carver (ed) *The Cross Goes North: Processes of Conversion in Northern Europe,* (Woodbridge)

Poulton, R. and Scott, E. 1993. 'The Hoarding, Deposition and Use of Pewter in Roman Britain' *Theoretical Roman Archaeology: First Conference Proceedings,* Aldershot, 115–132

Ross, A. 1968. 'Shafts, pits, wells – sanctuaries of the Belgic Britons?' in J.M. Coles and D.D.A. Simpson (eds) *Studies in Ancient Europe: Essays Presented to Stuart Piggot,* London

Scott, S. 2000.*Art and Society in Fourth-Century Britain: Villa Mosaics in Context,* (Oxford)

Swift, E. 2000. *The End of the Western Roman Empire,* (Stroud)

Toynbee, J.M.C. 1968. 'Pagan Motifs and Practices in Christian Art and Ritual in Roman Britain' in M.W. Barley and R.P.C. Hanson.(eds) *Christianity in Britain, 300-700,* (Leicester) , 177-92

Objects and sites

Appleshaw	Read, C.H. 1989. 'List of pewter dishes and vessels found at Appleshaw and now in the British Museum' *Archaeologia,* **56**, 7-12
Appleford	Brown. D. 1973 'A Romano Pewter Hoard from Appleford, Berkshire' *Oxoniensis,* **38**, 184-206
Belt buckles	Mawer 1995, 59-65
Canterbury	Johns, C.M. and Potter, T.W. 1985. 'The Canterbury Late Roman Treasure' *Antiquaries Journal* 65, 312-52
Bywell	Mawer 1995, 14; Haverfield, F. 1914. 'Roman Silver in Northumberland' *Journal Roman of Studies,* 4, 1-12
Corbridge	Mawer 1995, 17
Flawborough	Elliot, L. and Malone, S. 1998 `Flawborough lead tank' in 'Archaeology in Nottinghamshire 1998' *Transactions of the Thoroton Soc Nottinghamshire, 103,* 87–107
Frampton	Huskinson, J. 1974. 'Some pagan mythological figures and their significance in Early Christian art' *Papers of the British School of Rome,* 42, 68-97,
Hinton	See references in Chapter 1
Hockwold	Johns, C.M., 1986. 'The Roman Silver Cups from Hockwold, Norfolk' *Archaeologia* 108, 1-13
Icklingham	Liversidge, J. 1959. 'A New Hoard of Romano-British Pewter at Icklingham, Suffolk' *Proceedings of the Cambridge Antiquarian Society,* 52, 6-10

	Liversidge, J. 1962. 'A Bronze Bowl and other Vessels from Icklingham, Suffolk' *Proceedings of the Cambridge Antiquarian Society,* 55, 6-7
Ingots	Mawer 1995, 96-8
Long Wittenham	See reference in Chapter 1
Lullingstone	See reference in Chapter 1
North Stoke	Journal of Roman Studies 45 (1955), 147, no.15
Norton	YAJ
Mildenhall	See references in Chapter 1
Poundbury	Sparey-Green, C. 1993. 'The Mausolea Painted Plaster' in Farwell, D.E. and Molleson, T.I. *Poundbury Volume 2: The Cemeteries,* (Dorchester), 135-141
Rings	Mawer 1995, 65-77
Shavington	See reference in Chapter 2
Silchester	Boon, G.C. 1957. *Roman Siclhester: The Archaeology of a Romano-British Town,* (London)130, Fig.22
Traprain Law	See references in Chapter 1
Uley	See references in Chapter 3
Water Newton	See references in Chapter 1

Historical texts
Augustine, *The City of God* – H. Bettenson (trans. and ed.) London

6 Dying Christian

Brown, P, 1981. *The Cult of the Saints: Its Rise and Function in Latin Christianity,* (Oxford), 23-49

Handley, M. 2001. 'The Origins of Christian commemoration in late Antique Britain' *Early Medieval Europe* 10 (2), 177-99

Paxton, F.S., 1990. *Christianizing Death: The Creation of a Ritual Process,* (Ithaca)

Philpott, R., 1991. *Burial Practices in Roman Britain: A Survey of Grave Treatment and Furnishing,* British Archaeological Reports **219** (Oxford)

Quensel-von Kalbern, L., 1999. 'The British Church and the Emergence of the Anglo-Saxon Kingdoms' *Anglo-Saxon Studies in Archaeology and History*, **10**, 89–98

Todd, M. 1999. 'The Latest Inscriptions of Roman Britain' *Durham Archaeological Journal,* 14-15, 53-9

Objects and sites

Ashton	Frere, S., 1984. 'Roman Britain in 1983' *Britannia,* **15**, 265–332

Frere, S.S., 1985. 'Roman Britain in 1984' *Britannia,*
16, 251–317

Colchester See references in Chapter 1

Icklingham See references in Chapter 1

Ilchester Leach, P.J., 1982. *Ilchester Volume 1: Excavations 1974–5,*
(Bristol)

Leach, P.J., (ed.) 1994. *Ilchester Volume 2: Archaeology,*
Excavation and Fieldwork to 1984, (Sheffield)

Poundbury See references in Chapter 5

Winchester Clarke, G., 1979. *Winchester Studies 3. Pre-Roman and*
Roman Winchester Part II, The Roman Cemetery at
Lankhills, (Oxford)

Shepton- Mallet Leach, P. 2001. *Excavation of a Romano-British roadside*
settlement in Somerset: Fosse Lane, Shepton Mallet,
1990, (London)

Historical texts

Augustine *De cura gerenda pro mortuis,* - Lacey, J. (ed. and trans.)
'The care to be taken for the dead' in. *St. Augustine:*
Treatises on Marriage and Other Subjects: The Fathers of
the Church, **27** (New York,1955)

Augustine *The City of God* H. Bettenson (ed and trans.) London

Tertullian *De Resurrectione = Tertullian's Treatise on the Resurrection,*
ed. and trans. E. Evans (London; 1960)

Sulpicius Severus *The Life of Martin of Tours,* in White, C. (ed. and trans.)
Early Christian Lives, (London, 1998), 129-160

7 Conclusions

Bassett, S. 1982. 'Medieval Lichfield: a topographical review' *TSSAHS* 22,
95–8

Bassett, S. 1991. 'Churches in Worcester before and after the conversion of
the Anglo-Saxons' *Antiquities Journal,* 69, 225–56

Bassett, S. 1992. 'Medieval ecclesiastical organization in the vicinity of
Wroxeter and its British antecedents' *Journal of the British Archaeological*
Association, 145, 1–29

Bassett, S. 1992. 'Church and diocese in the West Midlands: the transition from
British to Anglo-Saxon control' in Blair, J. and Sharpe, R. (eds) *Pastoral Care*
Before the Parish, (Leicester), 13–40

Esmonde Cleary, S. 1989. *The Ending of Roman Britain,* (London)

Knight, J. 1999.*The End of Antiquity: Archaeology, Society and Religion AD235-*
700, (Stroud)

Historical texts
Marwnad Cynddylan   Kirby, D.P., 1977 'Welsh bards and the border' in
                     Cramp, R. (ed.) *Mercian Studies*, 31–42

Objects and sites
Christian Graffitti   Mawer 1995, 19, 34-42
Rings   Mawer 1995, 65-77

INDEX